The Shame of Southern Politics

The Shame of Southern Politics

Essays and Speeches

LESLIE DUNBAR

THE UNIVERSITY PRESS OF KENTUCKY

For Rachel and Sam

Publication of this volume was made possible in part
by a grant from the National Endowment for the Humanities.

Copyright © 2002 by The University Press of Kentucky

Scholarly publisher for the Commonwealth, serving Bellarmine University, Berea College, Centre College of Kentucky, Eastern Kentucky University, The Filson Historical Society, Georgetown College, Kentucky Historical Society, Kentucky State University, Morehead State University, Murray State University, Northern Kentucky University, Transylvania University, University of Kentucky, University of Louisville, and Western Kentucky University. All rights reserved.

Editorial and Sales Offices: The University Press of Kentucky
663 South Limestone Street, Lexington, Kentucky 40508-4008

06 05 04 03 02   1 2 3 4 5

Foreword from *Climbing Jacob's Ladder: The Arrival of Negroes in Southern Politics* by Pat Watters and Reese Cleghorn, copyright © 1967 by Southern Regional Council, Inc. and renewed 1995 by Southern Regional Council, Inc.
Reprinted by permission of Harcourt, Inc.

Frontispiece: Leslie Dunbar outside Dunbar, West Virginia, on one of his annual field trips to Appalachia, probably in the early 1970s.

Library of Congress Cataloging-in-Publication Data

Dunbar, Leslie.
The shame of southern politics : essays and speeches / Leslie Dunbar.
p. cm.
Includes bibliographical references.
ISBN 0-8131-2261-9 (cloth : alk. paper)
1. Dunbar, Leslie—Archives. 2. African Americans—Archives. 3. African American political activists—Archives. 4. African American civil rights workers—Archives.
5. Southern States—Politics and government—1951- —Sources. 6. Southern States—Race relations—Sources. 7. United States—Politics and government—1945-1989—Sources. 8. United States—Politics and government—1989- —Sources. 9. United States—Race relations—Sources. 10. African Americans—Civil rights—
History—20th century—Sources. I. Title.
E185.97.D83D86   2002
323.1'196073075'09045—dc21

2002010996

Contents

Introduction by Dan Carter
(2001)
viii

Preface
(2001)
xxiii

1
The Annealing of the South
(1961)
1

2
Civil Rights and Civil Duties
(1962)
15

3
The Changing Mind of the South: The Exposed Nerve
(1964)
25

4
An Excerpt from My Foreword to *Climbing Jacob's Ladder:*
The Arrival of Negroes in Southern Politics
(1967)
43

5
Remarks to the National Civil Liberties Clearing House
(1968)
49

6
Remarks to the Mississippi Council on Human Relations
(1975)
59

7
Remarks to the Southern Regional Council
(1977)
69

8
The South: Then and Now
(1978)
81

9
Excerpts from *Minority Report*
(1987)
93

10
Not by Law Alone: *Brown* in Retrospect
(1994)
107

11

What to Make of the Old Civil Rights Movement:
A Partial and Partisan View
(2000)
121

12

1968: A Reflection
(2001–2002)
141

Notes
169

Introduction

Dan Carter

For much of the last quarter century, the opening and closing bells of Wall Street have been the pacemaker of the American political and economic system. The unapologetic boast of Gordon Gekko ("Greed is good") may have been replaced by President George Bush's focus group–tested slogan of scripted compassion ("Leave no child behind"), but the political response to September 11, 2001, was a chilling object lesson in what really counts in today's politics. While the bagpipes were still playing at the funerals of middle-class public servants—police officers and firemen who had given the last full measure—the Washington lobbyists were swarming through the nation's capitol bullying (without much resistance) legislators into proposing still another multibillion-dollar tax cut to the very individuals who have already profited so handsomely during the last twenty years.

In these troubled times, more than ever, we need to hear the voice of Leslie Dunbar.

On one level, these essays need no introduction: the moral vision, the quiet decency, and the intense commitment spring from every page. It is the voice of the best of the American liberal tradition. These are not the words that the author of these essays would like to hear about himself for he is (as his friends and family will attest) a compulsively modest man. His son, Tony, has suggested that it is part of that upland heritage of reticence. I like to believe that natural modesty is strengthened by a lifetime of watching so-called leaders more interested in promoting their reputations than in building their causes. And yet I think it is important to recognize the extraordinary role that Leslie Dunbar has played in the struggles to create a different, more humane America.

He was born, as he likes to say, on Mozart's birthday, 1921, in Lewisburg, West Virginia. One of the oldest towns west of the Alleghenies, it was part of western Virginia that seceded from the Confederacy and formed a new union state in 1863. But Lewisburg, site of a brief but fierce engagement between Federal and Confederate forces in May of 1862, was a hotbed of antiunion sympathy and showed little enthusiasm for the free state of West Virginia. The monument in the town square was Confederate and "all the trappings . . . were Southern," Dunbar has recalled. His background was comfortably middle class as he spent the first eight years of his life on one of the tree-shaded streets of Lewisburg. While the road not traveled will always be a mystery, it is possible that, had the depression not intervened, Dunbar might never have left. But the depression wiped out his father's business in 1929 and sent the family to Baltimore, where his mother ran a boardinghouse and his father struggled to adapt to a world turned upside down.

Baltimore was an altogether different environment. The boarders at his family's rooming house were one part of his education, he recalled, and the other ("the best schooling I ever got") was at Baltimore City College (actually a high school) and the Enoch Pratt Free Library.[1] Despite the fact that he was married and soon had a child, when the war began in 1941 he badly wanted to join the army and unsuccessfully appealed his 4-F classification. And so he attended the University of Maryland and worked the night shift at a local aircraft assembly plant. After receiving a Ph.D. in political science from Cornell in 1948, he took a position at Emory University in Atlanta, where he began his lifelong involvement in the life of the American South.

In 1948, Emory was a small, struggling Methodist university with lofty ambitions but few resources. An assistant professorship might have supported a traditional bachelor scholar, but it was precious little, as Dunbar ruefully recalled, for a married man with two children. He became director of community affairs at the Aiken H-Bomb plant in the early 1950s, received a prestigious Guggenheim fellowship in 1954, and then after a short stint teaching at Mount Holyoke returned to Atlanta to join the staff of the Southern Regional Council (SRC).[2]

The biracial (but predominantly white) Council was a reincarnated version of the old Atlanta-based Commission on Interracial Cooperation founded in 1919. The old CIC had drawn most of its membership from the ranks of educators, journalists, and religious leaders, and it was not without accomplishments. The women's division under Jessie Daniel Ames had been an effective force in helping to fight lynching in the 1920s and 1930s, and the organization maintained tenuous connections between black and white Southerners in the quarter century after its creation, no small feat in a society that was racially segregated from birth to death. But most of its white members accepted "separate but equal" as the natural order of race relations. Whatever their good intentions, they were firmly committed to working within a paternalistic tradition. Certainly there was little interest in challenging the foundations of racial discrimination.

By the early 1940s, black (and some white) Southerners were no longer willing to accept the Commission's timidity. Between 1942 and 1944, it was replaced by the Southern Regional Council, and after initially temporizing on the issue the Council endorsed racial desegregation in 1951, a move which led to a drastic reduction in membership during the mid-1950s.

Dunbar arrived in 1958 to become the SRC's director of research just as the organization—under the leadership of Harold Fleming—was on the rebound. Under Fleming, the SRC had quietly worked—often behind the scenes—to help local communities resolve increasing racial tensions. At the same time, Dunbar coordinated a number of studies highlighting the future of the region as well as the problems caused by the continuation of patterns of poverty and racial tension. In today's context, the SRC of the early 1960s would seem to have been a cautious and conservative organization, hardly deserving of the bitter attacks made by segregationist politicians and organizations like the Citizens' Councils.

Much of that work continued, but Dunbar—in his quiet way—took a much more active personal role in the accelerating civil rights movement. These were years of change for him as well. Before the late-

1950s he had thought about the issues of race and poverty, but when he became director of research for SRC, he set out to prepare a study of racial inequities in Atlanta, working side by side with Carl Holman. Holman was the first black person with whom he had worked as an equal. They became close friends and, as Dunbar would recall, Holman became "one of my earliest teachers about the actualities, not merely the forms, of American race relations."[3] During these same years, his close friendship with Sam and Sylvia Cook and other members of Atlanta's black community gave him an insight into those "actualities" of race relations.

And he quickly came to see that, though the interwoven issues of race and poverty were endemic in the South, they were also national problems. In 1981, Dunbar's son, Tony, wrote the provocative book *Against the Grain: Southern Radicals and Prophets, 1929–1959*. He must have had his father in mind, for Leslie Dunbar seemed to spend much of his career challenging the reigning political and intellectual assumptions. In 1957, in a piece not included in this collection, he wrote his first essay on race relations in the South at a time when whites in the region were most fearful, most angry, and most defiant in the face of *Brown v. Board of Education*. In 1956, goaded by Richmond *News Leader* editor James J. Kilpatrick, the state of Virginia had endorsed the doctrine of "interposition," an assertion of state sovereignty and supremacy that had been repudiated decisively at Appomattox in 1865. Eight other Southern state legislatures soon fell into line with an endorsement of this absurd doctrine while all but a handful of U.S. Senators and Representatives signed a "Declaration of Constitutional Principles" in March of 1956 bitterly attacking the *Brown* decision as "contrary to the Constitution." By 1957, the "Citizens' Council" movement—reinforced by violence and mob actions—had bludgeoned white moderates into silence and most of the Southern states had threatened to close the public schools rather than allow even token desegregation.

And yet Dunbar rejected the notion that the South fundamentally was different from the rest of the nation (and irredeemable). His 1957 essay spoke with cautious optimism about the future of race relations in the region. And the first essay in this collection, "The Annealing of the South," moved against the truisms of what passed for conventional wisdom in 1961. While segregationists continued to warn that integration would lead to the flow of "blood in the streets" and cautious national leaders held back because of political timidity, Dunbar boldly predicted that once the fight for segregation was "decisively lost," the "typical white Southerner will shrug his shoulders, resume his stride, and go on."

When Dunbar succeeded Fleming as executive director in 1961, the organization began to take an even more active role in the civil rights struggle. These were years of whirlwind activity, and civil rights activists often turned to him for support both publicly and privately. In 1961, it was Dunbar who suggested to Sam Cook that they arrange an introduction between Martin Luther King Jr. and the influential Atlanta newspaper editor Ralph McGill. As Cook noted, the friendship between the two men began that night in his living room and grew stronger over the years. Despite McGill's initial cautious approach to racial change, his growing friendship with King gave the civil rights movement a supportive voice in the South's most prominent newspaper.

In 1963, when the National Council of Churches began to withdraw support from Will Campbell, the iconoclastic Baptist preacher and Southern gadfly, Dunbar used his influence with the Field Foundation to obtain a grant that allowed Campbell to continue his work as head of an ad hoc Committee of Southern Churchmen. That same year, he broke SRC tradition by sponsoring a special report which criticized the Federal Bureau of Investigation for failing to protect civil rights workers in Albany, Georgia, and (by implication) other parts of the South—this at a time when J. Edgar Hoover and the Bureau were still regarded as fearless crime fighters, exempt from public scrutiny.

And it was Dunbar who played a decisive role in supporting University of Mississippi historian James Silver when he decided to challenge the climate of repression that gripped his state with a speech before the Southern Historical Association in November of 1963. Dunbar encouraged Silver to go public and arranged a commercial publisher for Silver's personal account of his experiences, *Mississippi: The Closed Society*.[4]

Despite occasional setbacks and some difficult moments (particularly in the Deep South), the forceful action of civil rights activists had turned the tide by the late 1950s; segregation was on the retreat, a retreat which became a full-scale rout with the passage of the Civil Rights Act of 1964 and the Voting Rights Act of 1965.

That same year, Dunbar left the SRC to become head of the Field Foundation. Marshall Field, the millionaire retailer and philanthropist who established the foundation in 1940, was a pioneer in supporting civil rights and antipoverty. For Steve Suitts, who later served as executive director of the SRC, Dunbar's risk-taking and creativity initiated a unique period in American philanthropy and the Field Foundation made an impact out of proportion to its size and assets. Thirty years later, those individuals who had an inside view of Dunbar's quiet but focused creativity at the Field Foundation still remember with a mixture of affection and admiration the leadership he offered to movements for social change. He had an ability to sit through long meetings, asking a few questions, listening intently. At some point, recalls Will Campbell, he would begin speaking in his quiet, almost inaudible voice and give shape and direction to often ill-formed ideas and alternatives. "Of course, by the next day, everyone there was convinced they had formulated the final plans and recommendations," says Campbell.

His strategy was simple: respond quickly to creative grassroots projects that had the potential for mobilizing citizens on important social problems. He had, as everyone agrees, a remarkable ability to size up the strengths and weaknesses of individuals. If the project held promise and the individuals who proposed it could be trusted, he supported it with a minimum of red tape and then stepped out of the way. The names of those he supported reads like an honor roll of social activists who struggled to transform our nation: Wiley Branton (who was the first head of SRC's Voter Education Project); Cesar Chavez, whose crusade for Hispanic migrant workers helped move the civil rights movement from black and white to black, white, and brown; Marian Wright Edelman, who went on to found the Children's Defense Fund; William Velasquez, who created the Southwest Voter Registration and Education Project; Gerald Wilkinson, one of the founders of the National Indian Youth Council; and John Lewis. (After black power advocates deposed SNCC Chairman John Lewis, Dunbar arranged for his appointment to the Field Foundation staff while he finished his degree.)

Through these and other individuals and groups, the Field Foundation continued its emphasis upon civil rights in small and larger ways. The Foundation gave critical early support to voting rights campaigns. Other grants were instrumental in supporting the early stages of legal services and childhood development in the South and projects dealing with hunger in America. Long before the links between racism and the criminal justice system were widely understood, Dunbar had supported work by a special Committee for the Study of Incarceration. The findings were published in 1976 as *Doing Justice: The Choice of Punishments*.

At the same time, his interests were not simply focused on the South and race. Among other projects, the Field Foundation's grant to David and Sheila Rothman allowed them to undertake their study of New York's massive Willowbrook State Mental Hospital, a project that played a powerful role in the demise of the massive institutions that had earlier been created for the treatment of mental illness in America.[5]

The Foundation also sought to address the nexus between race, poverty, and political powerlessness. In 1962, in an essay reprinted in this collection ("Civil Rights and Civil Duties"), he reminded a New York audience that the issue was more than simply a matter of ending legal segregation in the South: the "hardest wrought issues of civil rights concern those whom an earlier and more romantic generation would have called the down-trodden masses." In the tenements of Harlem and the back alleys of other cities and towns, in the impoverished worn-out land of the rural South, in the camps of migrant workers and in invisible nooks and crannies all over America lived people for whom "the American standard of living, the American way of life, the affluent society, are but the emptiest of phrases." It was a theme to which he returned throughout his career, and the problems of massive inequality are the bass notes of all these essays.

That emphasis upon the importance of economic justice reinforced his suspicion of political struggle based upon racial identity. It was not simply that he believed integration was morally correct, but he was convinced that so-called racial problems could only be addressed by creating coalitions that united people across the color line. As he said in 1977: "Unemployment, bad schooling, and crime are not racial problems, no matter how many blacks or Hispanics may be trapped in them. They are national problems, residues of inequitable political and economic systems, and the responsibility of all of us." Still, he had no illusions that achieving that cross-racial coalition would be easy. While he hoped that the introduction of black voters into Southern politics would revitalize the civic life of the region, he also foresaw—as early as 1964—the danger that the deeply entrenched conservatism of the traditional South would blend with that of national conservatism.

For those who had succeeded in destroying segregation and creating new political and economic opportunities for black Southerners, these were years of hope and promise. Only with the advantage of hindsight can we see the strength of the obstacles they faced. In the 1950s and 1960s, the news media focused upon white Southerners' angry defense of legal segregation, but many white Northerners also opposed civil rights, particularly when it involved issues such as neighborhood housing and greater access to jobs. As the struggle moved beyond ending *de jure* segregation and black disfranchisement, the fragile national consensus on civil rights dissolved. Many of the white Americans who were enthusiastic about attacking racial discrimination so long as it remained a "Southern" issue were far less enthusiastic once "civil rights" was broadened to include a critical examination of patterns of residential segregation and systemic forms of economic and educational discrimination—problems that existed in the North as well as the South. At the same time, the urban race riots of the mid-1960s galvanized white backlash while the war divided the left and isolated it from many of its most powerful constituencies. American liberals—particularly those interested in matters of race—often seemed adrift and uncertain over how to take the movement to the next stage.

Dunbar was always conscious of the tenuous nature of this national support for civil rights, and he was one of the first observers to understand just how divisive and wounding were the White House Conferences on Civil Rights held in November 1965 and May 1966. Those public forums, he wrote in early 1967, "forced people who desperately and above all, at that period, needed a private time to find new thoughts, to nag at each other in a lurid spotlight, and to drag down a lovely, cleanly phrased movement into a whirlpool of sullen meaningless talk...." We had entered, he warned, an era of "the chant rather than the song, of the incantation rather than the thought...."

By the mid-1970s, the Field Foundation's Board—encouraged by Foundation president Morris B. Abram—had begun to express its lack of enthusiasm for several key projects supported by Dunbar. Triggered by his soul-searching over the war in Vietnam, Dunbar had begun to look much more critically at the international as well as domestic policies of the United States in the 1960s and 1970s. Like Martin Luther King Jr., he had become convinced there was an inescapable link between domestic and international policy. In the mid-1970s, the Field Foundation awarded grants to the Center for Defense Information (CDI) and the Center for National Security Studies (CNSS). Scholars and experts at the CDI challenged many of the orthodoxies of cold war military strategy and highlighted the role of the United States in arms proliferation around the world. In the wake of the abuses highlighted by the Watergate affair, the Center for National Security Studies (CNSS) sought to monitor and challenge government agencies when they used "national security" as a justification for the abuse of civil liberties.

While some members of the board were unhappy over these grants, matters came to a head in 1980 after Dunbar proposed that the Foundation support an antidraft organization and continue funding a study by the Institute for Policy Studies on the role of the United States in armaments transfers. (The Institute, like the CDI and the CNSS, was often critical of American foreign policy, particularly in developing countries.) Abram led the way in blocking the two grants and he made it clear that the board of directors did not share Dunbar's concerns over American foreign policy. The United States, he said, was "one of the most moral of nation states." Dunbar resigned, a move that triggered a front-page story in the *New York Times*.

From Field, he moved to several teaching posts and consultancies until he went to work in 1985 for the Ford Foundation for two years, a period he has bluntly described as one of the most miserable in his life. The Ford Foundation had far more resources than Field, but with its size also came a cumbersome and often impenetrable bureaucracy. Drawing upon his long experience in dealing with issues of race, poverty, and education—traditional concerns of the Foundation—Dunbar and his fellow senior associate Mitchell Ginsburg outlined plans for action that—he soon discovered—disappeared into the labyrinth of the upper floors of the organization. Without support from the Foundation's executives, he resigned in 1983.

The cautiousness of the nation's foundations mirrored the increasing conservatism of the American electorate. Through the 1960s and even the 1970s, there were measurable improvements in the quality of life for many minorities in the nation. And Jimmy Carter's administration, for all its disappointments, did elevate the issue of human rights in American foreign policy. For Dunbar, as for most supporters of social justice, however, Ronald Reagan's election in 1980 ushered in a bleak decade.

With an updated version of the Southern strategy that Barry Goldwater and Richard Nixon had developed in the 1960s and early 1970s, Reagan sought to build a Republican majority upon the foundations of traditional right-wing economic policies, white backlash (North and South), and a bellicose foreign policy that divided the world in Manichean fashion between good and evil. Throughout the developing world, the Reagan administration propped up unsavory right-wing regimes and expanded the nation's role as the leading exporter of arms. The results of those policies had their most malevolent impact in Central America, where right-wing terror squads in Guatemala and Honduras systematically imprisoned, tortured, and murdered "leftist" opponents while American officials turned a blind eye or (in some cases) actively encouraged their actions in the name of anticommunism. While the Reagan administration carried on its illegal support of the Contras in El Salvador, it lied to Congress and the American people as it sought—often with the ineptness of Keystone Cops—to engage in illegal arms dealing with the Iranian government.

Meanwhile at home, Reagan attacked the social net for the disadvantaged with the same enthusiasm that he supported right-wing regimes abroad. On the grounds that government efforts to end poverty in the 1960s and 1970s had been a "failure," the Reagan administration embraced laissez-faire capitalism as the solution to problems of poverty. Prosperity would "trickle down" from the wealthy to the poor.

His economic advisers made no effort to conceal their belief that their most important goal was to reduce any sense of entitlement on the part of the poor while dramatically reducing tax rates on the wealthy.

Through the 1980s and into the 1990s, a new generation of right-wing ideologues assembled the intellectual scaffolding for the new order. The common link that united all these ideas—whether the bizarre supply-side economics of Arthur Laffer or the proudly cynical conflation of law and economics by Richard Posner of the Chicago school of legal jurisprudence—was the worship of the marketplace. And underlying it all was an unspoken assumption: if you make the lives of the poor, the working class, and the marginal middle class more precarious and give them less money, they will be more productive and resourceful workers, returning benefits to society as a whole. And then if you give the rich and the well-to-do more money and make their already prosperous lives even more secure, they will be more productive and resourceful in returning benefits to society as a whole.

The problem, as Dunbar pointed out in 1984, was that the notion of a "free market" in the United States had always been a fantasy. Since the nineteenth century, vested economic interests had made sure that political decisions always accommodated their interests. "In short," he said, they have "insisted upon their *entitlements*."[6]

The end result of such ideological fantasy was what one would expect. Few undertakings are as fraught with statistical peril as an attempt to isolate the effect of Reaganomics on the declining economic condition of low-income Americans in general—and black Americans specifically—during the 1980s. There were a number of other factors: the internationalization of trade and the decline of high-paying blue-collar jobs (accompanied by the decline of trade unions), and the technological disruption of the labor market. At the same time, the large number of one-parent households, particularly in the nation's black community, exacerbated other negative economic forces.

Nevertheless, it is irrefutable that government policy reinforced that process. Despite all the talk of tax cuts, the policies of the Reagan administration brought significant benefits to a minority of the population. The bottom 50 percent actually saw tax increases as social security and excise levies more than offset marginal declines in the income tax rates. Those between the fiftieth and ninetieth percentile experienced relatively little change. In contrast, the closer to the top of the pyramid, the greater the reduction in the effective federal tax rates. The top 10 percent enjoyed a 5 percent cut in taxes; the top 1 percent, a 15 percent cut, even as the administration tenaciously sought reductions in need-based programs for the very poor.[7]

In the early 1990s, Dunbar summarized the inevitable results. Between 1980 and 1987, he noted, the percentage of all income held by the upper fifth increased 5 percent, while those in the lowest fifth saw their share of the national income decline 10 percent.[8] And most of that shift went to the very richest, a process, we might add, which has continued through the 1990s. In inflation-corrected dollars, the top 1 percent has seen its after-tax income increase 120 percent in the last quarter century, the bottom 20 percent has actually suffered a decline of 12 percent in after-tax income. Thirty million Americans—more than half of them children—still live below the poverty line; forty-three million Americans still have no health insurance. And despite the last ten years of steady economic expansion—once you exclude increased family income due to the growing number of dual wage earners—it was only in 1997 that childhood poverty had a slight decline and the mid-50 percent of households in America saw an equally small increase in income, improvements likely to be swept away as the economy slows.

While all lower income Americans suffered during the 1980s, blacks as a group were hit hardest by the combination of structural changes in the economy. The adoption of low-income tax credits only partially offset the more significant negative impact of changes in the tax structure and reductions in levels of federal welfare. As Thomas and Mary Edsall concluded in their book *Chain Reaction*, middle- to upper-income African Americans have had a steady if unspectacular improvement in their earnings throughout the 1970s and 1980s. But the bottom 10 percent—already desperately poor—experienced an 18 percent decline in family income between 1979 and 1987. By 1990, blacks in the bottom 20 percent of the nation's population were poorer in relation to whites than at any time since the 1950s.[9]

Despite his disappointment over the rightward turn in American politics, as these essays make clear, Dunbar continued to speak and to keep alive the concerns that had formed the core of his life. The 1984 book he edited, *Minority Report: What Has Happened to Blacks, Hispanics, American Indians, & Other Minorities in the Eighties*, documents the continuing disadvantages suffered by African Americans, Hispanics, American Indians, and other minorities, and he eloquently rejected the fundamental assumption that underlay much of Reaganomics: the notion that the inability of the antipoverty programs of the 1960s and 1970s to reach their ultimate goal should lead to their eradication. "What ever does work, once and for all?" he asked.[10] What was clear was that the timid, poorly funded antipoverty programs had ameliorated conditions; the solution was not to abandon them, but to refine, expand, and improve their effectiveness. In 1988, he tried to show how this might be done in his book *The Common Interest: How Our Social Welfare Policies Don't Work and What We Can Do About Them.*

Three years later, he published *Reclaiming Liberalism*, an ambitious attempt to go to the philosophical roots of this increasingly scorned tradition. *Reclaiming Liberalism* was a deeply personal book that grew out of his conviction that the two great enemies he had come to oppose in his life, the military and poverty, were inextricably interwoven. The "present tasks of liberals and the present meaning of liberalism are to oppose militarism and to measure every public policy against the question *What does this mean for the poor?*" His book, he said, was a "meditation on that proposition."

Reclaiming Liberalism was idiosyncratic in form (when measured against the comfortable intellectual conventions that had come to dominate ideologues of left and right), undogmatic and open-minded. By their nature, he argued, liberals had to live in the midst of an unsettling assumption: "Certainty is our undoing." (No maxim is unconditional, he once wrote, "except possibly to practice kindness.") The "early Christians, early Protestants, early Marxists, all had their own 'good news' for the world," concluded Dunbar, "but each also flung certainties among their believers that led to inquisitions and gulags. God help us from true believers."[11]

Although he never embraced dogma or final answers, he did conclude that there were six rights necessary for justice and liberty (and order and stability) in modern societies:

> The right to have and pursue a vocation.

> The right to own property.
> The right to live in dignity.
> . . . .
> The right to dissent from authority
> The right to live under a rule of law.
> The right to be let alone.[12]

And he argued the case for these rights in this wide-ranging book that moved between a thoughtful exposition of classical political theory and lessons derived from concrete, lived experiences. But seldom was there a case more inopportunely argued. Dunbar finished *Reclaiming Liberalism* on the eve of the outbreak of the Gulf War in 1991. By the time it appeared, the American people were swept up in the patriotic fervor of the moment, and there was little inclination to ponder the perils of militarism as marching columns of troops returned home to cheering crowds. Despite the fact that the prestigious publisher W.W. Norton released the book, it received only a brief (though positive) notice in *Choice* and an extended appreciative review by Harry Ashmore in the *Virginia Quarterly*.

In spite of the lack of public response to *Reclaiming Liberalism*, Dunbar continued to write and speak. After he retired and moved to Durham, North Carolina, he became active in his community, quietly playing a key role in promoting local projects that addressed his long-time concerns over war and militarism, poverty and racism. And to those he added a new emphasis upon the need to confront homophobia and to protect our natural environment.

In his usual self-deprecating manner, Leslie Dunbar has often said that—as an habitual pessimist—he is often seen as a prophet. But he underestimates his own record. No one writing in the midst of the passions and commitments of the last half century could always be right, but he has been correct more than almost anyone who lived through these years.

In *On the Good Life*, the Roman philosopher and orator Cicero reflected on what he believed to be the three divisions of moral goodness: the ability to distinguish "truth from falsity" and to understand the relationship between "one phenomenon and another and the causes and consequences of each one"; the habits of self-discipline that allow one to "restrain the passions"; and the willingness to always "behave considerately and understandingly in our associations with other people." Those who know Leslie Dunbar would never suggest that he has been a dispassionate man, but his passions have not been the kind of self-indulgent follies Cicero had in mind: blind and thoughtless anger, envy, arrogance and greed. His essays in this collection make clear the ways in which his deep emotional commitments have always turned outward, toward the creation of a just society in which the weak would be protected and the powerful restrained. And he has certainly fulfilled Cicero's admonition that moral goodness must rest upon a truth-telling that is in turn founded upon a profound understanding of the causes and consequences of all our actions.

As I view the current political climate, there are moments when I wonder if the battle has been lost, if the struggles of my life, and of those I have known and admired, for a more democratic, egalitarian, and humane society are simply a mask of self-delusion that conceals the human animal's compulsion to maximize those forms of self-interest that today's conservative ideologues seem to find so comforting. What keeps me going is the powerful example of men and women like Leslie Dunbar, who spent their lives battling the assumption aptly characterized and justly scorned by the Puritan martyr Richard Rumbold that "Providence had sent a few men into the world, ready booted and spurred to ride, and millions ready saddled and bridled to be ridden."

He has maintained a steadfastness that shames us all by example and he has lived long enough to remind us that authentic political movements have emerged when least expected. Who could have predicted the great achievement of Social Security in 1929? And who could have anticipated in 1948 that we were on the verge of an all-out assault on segregation. The women and men who challenged Jim Crow in the 1930s and 1940s faced far more daunting obstacles than those we now confront. Political movements begin at the grassroots level and have their greatest impact when we least expect it. It is always hard to predict where, when, or how the next movement for social justice will coalesce and emerge, but Leslie Dunbar's writings and the example he gave us are powerful weapons in helping us begin to reclaim the hope for a more equitable society that once inspired a generation.

Preface

I would like to claim for this book, despite its many mistaken analyses and so much of importance having been left out, that it is nevertheless true to the spirit of the citizen reform movements of the late 1950s, the 1960s, and the 1970s, and that it grasps some portion of their essential features.

From my many essays, I chose ones that seem not only true to their times but connected to our present. Each is preceded by an introductory comment.

The civil rights movement was one of the ennobling periods in our nation's history. I was not one of its principal figures, certainly not one of its leaders. If the whole of it might be conceived of as one single great enterprise, I might be considered a branch manager. But from my posts at the Southern Regional Council and the Field Foundation I served it.

Much that we strove for then seems to me to be now at risk, and in especially great risk since September 11, 2001. If there is or is to be international community, the brutish actions of that day cannot be tolerated. My own hope was that the response to these Al-Qaeda and allied terrorists not be through military force. The world is now awash in deaths and destruction brought on through its omnipresent wars, and the thought of adding to that is hateful. Besides, the results of wars are hardly ever what was intended, nor are they likely to be in this one. Terrorism will not disappear from Earth while masses of its men and women can see no, or too little, clear paths for satisfying their human wants and hopes. Nevertheless, something must be done in response to the chain of terror that, so far, has climaxed with the attacks of September 11.

There are no mitigating conditions on that conclusion, none that could possibly justify what was done. But this is an unbalanced world at the beginning of the twenty-first century. Inequalities of wealth, of power, of military strength, of privileges of races (it is still mainly white people who rule the world), and of religions are all breeders of understandable resentments and hatreds.

Those inequalities can also not be long tolerated. Nor will they be indefinitely. The twenty-first century will not be a calm and peaceful one. The eleventh of September may have many cousins yet to be heard from.

We would have a better chance of deterring them and of ameliorating those inequalities if this declared war on terrorism were not presented as a war between good and evil, or between civilized nations and barbarians. There is no need for that.

I suppose that somewhere in this land there are persons at work already studying whether this war is a "just war." There usually have been, during and after our numerous wars. Some of the present-day analysts—possibly all in the near aftermath—will find, as has usually been found, that it is just, that it does meet the criteria propounded centuries ago by St. Augustine and later by St. Thomas Aquinas. President Bush's father had fastened on those criteria in an address on January 28, 1990, before the National Religious Broadcasters Convention, although they were not persuasive to all. A generally forgotten fact about *that* President Bush's war, against Iraq, was the strong opposition to it of so many—in fact, most—of the church bodies and church leaders who spoke out.[1]

Where will they stand this time? It is certain that they cannot be silent, because the war against terrorism has been, unfortunately, so forcefully cast as a fight between good and evil. And that is the territory of the churches, synagogues, and temples if anything is.

I probably have spent too much time, as a boy and a man, in church (and in studying the philosophers) to let these words, these old friends, good and evil, pass by without pause. Every ism, from concepts of terrorism to those of theism, is a human creation. Theism is that ism which most abundantly has birthed the definitions of what is good and what is evil and, even prior to the definitions, the very belief that good and evil are forces actively at work in the human world. In words eerily like his son's, the first President Bush had said of the soon-to-be-waged war against Iraq: "It has everything to do with what religion embodies—good versus evil, right versus wrong, human dignity and freedom versus tyranny and oppression. The war in the Gulf is not a Christian war, a Jewish war, or a Moslem war—it is a just war. And it is a war in which good will prevail."

Holy wars, whether Crusades preached by medieval Popes or by Moslem caliphs and mullahs or by American presidents, frighten me. They all require the suspension of what a fine American, Alexander Meiklejohn, rightly saw as one of the two basic principles of what we enjoy as a civilization: "be intelligent and act critically."[2] We are, when in a holy war, all too likely to be expected to think as we are told to think and to leave the critical thinking for a much later day. Religion may by now be secularized enough so that we can have, if we so desire, a holy war without the blessing of clergy. The early and all-conquering popularity of the war against Iraq, once underway, may have shown political leaders that they can lead the religious, that they, unaided except by followers, can pronounce good and evil.

Between the victims and the perpetrators of these modern terrorists' acts the issue is not religion (they have theirs, we have ours, both theistic) but something more universal: morality. The moral judgment is, rightfully, independent of religion. For free men and women—beings intelligent, critical, and kind—that is true now and has always been. Morality and "holy wars" are strangers to each other.

The menace of war is, however, only made fiercer by proclaiming it "holy." The values served by war are primeval and, consequently, self-justifying. As long as wars are fought by states, the value-question stipulated by Secretary of State Powell and others is as correct as any—essentially it is, can we win? Wars are for political ends. I think there are better and surer ways to those ends, but that is often a minority opinion.

A "war" against terror is a war for order. Without order, it will be contended, and probably correctly so, less fundamental principles such as liberty, equality, and all their derivatives could not take root and flourish. Order is to states as life is to individuals. A coalition of states, some of them strange allies indeed, can be assembled,[3] because terrorism, like anarchy, of which it is a bastard form, is enemy of all states. And that is probably true, though what history documents, and not just in the West, is that without those softer principles order doesn't last. But while it does, a war for order—which is always and necessarily a war without foreseen end—puts an end to democracy's laboriously arrived at standards for the behavior of states toward each other. A war for order may be perpetual war. Who could ever say when it is won?

So I hope (against hope, as the saying goes) that this talk of "just war" and good and evil can be muted, even shut down. Human beings, standing on their own moral feet, as it were, can well enough give themselves a secular aim. Defense of the international community and protection of human lives are sufficient causes. The proclamation of a holy war (or a "just war," which turns out to be much the same thing) is to take another long step, *very long*, toward identifying religion with patriotism, and that is inevitably to subordinate one to the other.

September 11 was neither Alpha nor Omega. On the day after, and all those since, the world had the same problems as before. We had, still, throughout Earth immense poverty, gross inequalities, and rancid racial discrimination, here at home the brutality of the death penalty, and still everywhere our natural environment crying for protection. We still had wars and threats of war worldwide. All of this had preceded Osama bin Laden. We had before and after, in short, civilization's continuing work to do.

September 2001

The above are conditions which only seldom do state governments of the South try to improve, and almost never do the South's Congressional delegations. There have been rare and brilliant exceptions among governors and congressmen. I can think of a score or so since World War II. More usually, they have been barriers to a more just democracy. That is a constant theme of the essays that follow, and so I speak of the shame of southern politics.

1

The Annealing of the South

1961

The first piece I published about civil rights issues appeared in the magazine America *on January 19, 1957, with the title "The South Will Move." I like that title, for at that time there was widespread belief to the contrary. I had asserted that "the South may move toward racial integration; it may move toward a kind of racial coexistence; it* will *move." The 1961 article reproduced below continued that claim.*

The second paragraph of this article seems to me about right even forty years later. Much has changed in the South, but in these fundamentals too much of the change, except in race relations, has been superficial and in degrees. On the other hand, although the political alliance between the old Black Belt and the "moneyed interests of the region's cities," which I mention farther on, still holds, the leadership of it comes now more definitely from the wealthy of the cities.

This article was correct in its belief that the old South was about to "lose again" and in its recognition that what Negro Southerners would win in the way of equality would be owed chiefly to themselves. I am afraid that it is not yet clear that the old South will not "win the peace," or at least a big share of it. A theme that will run through all the articles collected here is that southern politics from the Civil War to the present has wretchedly served southern people—and not only African Americans but all Southerners.

Nevertheless, I do not disavow the essay's concluding paragraphs. The region is far from the hoped-for society the civil rights movement hungered for. But the two races do live together with increasing respect for each other, and that is not a small achievement.

The article contains some out-of-date data (as will later reprints), but much of them are suggestively like present-day data; so too are some of the observations, such as one regarding crime and juvenile delinquency. The piece was originally written for an Italian journal and describes some matters that its readers could not be assumed to know.

Anneal: to subject to high heat, with subsequent cooling, for the purpose of softening thoroughly and rendering less brittle. In some cases, as for glass and steel, the cooling must be gradual; in others, as for copper and brass, it may be sudden. It is believed that annealing reduces brittleness by removing strains that have been induced in the material by some previous treatment. (*Webster's New International Dictionary*, 2nd edition.)

Now the land of fitful somnolence and passion nears the trap of reason. Even while it lashes at its captor, an air of anticipation courses pleasurably through the South at the prospect of the end of the long chase. The South is about to go down again in defeat, and can hardly wait.

The region has been the place where American error and excess go to retire. The most enormous of all, Negro enslavement and peonage, came here to live out its suffering. But this was not the only one. That part of the old frontier spirit which was crude and violent settled and, in some measure, still endures here. Obstinate localism, which is the other side of responsible local self-government, flourished like a tough weed. Wastefulness of the soil, its minerals and trees, always and everywhere an American sin, was most acute here where nature had given so lavishly. A late convert to laissez-faire economics, the South is slowest, perhaps, of all American regions to relinquish it emotionally. That Puritanism should have been received by Southerners seems almost implausible; but even before the chastening of the Civil War it had been, and it is still strong. The American dislike of theory which so impressed de Tocqueville is probably more virulent in the South than anywhere else.

This land of castoffs has been a maligned society and has, in truth, deserved most of its infamy. Yet it has been and is a beloved society as well, and from its punishing accumulation of hardship and error has somehow woven a life for its people which has not been without richness, and has not bereft men of self-respect. Possibly, just because Southerners are the only Americans who have known the agony of defeat and who have lived constantly with the reminder of their own moral guilt, there may be within them reservoirs of maturity and compassion that are not second in depth. Whites and Negroes, astonishingly like each other in beliefs and manners and attitudes, in sins and in virtues, have created, through the fires of history which have burned away much that is not essential beastliness and goodness in human nature, a society loved deeply by those who live within it.

The South has numerous definitions. It is best thought of as the states of the old Confederacy. In what Americans call the border states there are, however, sections where Southern characteristics and problems are as strong as anywhere, and one non-seceding state in particular—Kentucky—has a general resemblance. Moreover, there are parts of the South as here defined which bear little of the Southern stamp: western Texas is a land to itself, and southern Florida and northern Virginia are rapidly migrating northward in attitude and appearances. In fact, the South has never been all of one piece. There have been variations and fundamental differences of outlook. Nevertheless, there was a unity and it endures, though creakily. There has been the common remembrance of defeat and humiliation and economic inferiority, the common problem of a bi-racial population. There is a resulting sense of history which is more omnipresent than elsewhere in America; there is, as well, a common consent in the misreading of certain lessons and, worst of all, facts of history. And because of their history, and because they live close to it, Southerners have an awareness of their land and of the sanctity of "places" which is rare in this country. The land is as varied as nature could make it, and yet it and its imagery are a single strand in Southern self-consciousness: mountain ridges blend with moss-draped bayous, the heat-laden pine woods with undulating sand hills, the cotton manors fuse with the green valleys where yeomen make their crops, all in a single picture that has haunted and inspirited the Southerner for generations.

In the years following the Civil War, Henry Grady, a Georgian, proclaimed the "New South"; about every decade since, someone has again announced its coming. It comes; but then, of course, so does change everywhere and at all times. It has come but slowly, though now (did it seem so to Grady also?) it seems ready to burst in. That which has delayed change, while at the same time strengthening self-identity, has been the centrality of the racial issue. It has been the tether, limiting the distance which the region could move toward a political, economic, or social similarity with the rest of the nation. After the Civil War, white Southerners united in the conviction that the pre-eminent task was to maintain racial separateness and white superiority. So necessary was this seen to be, that all other concerns of society had to support it, and be subordinated to it. And so it has been. Political, economic, religious, educational institutions—all had to make their contributions to the dominating racial policy, and shape their own development in its interest.

Furthermore, though the tether had varying lengths in the differing sections of the South, at every time of crisis it tended to the marginal—the shortest-length, that of the so-called Black Belt. This is the old plantation country, descending in a great arc from southside Virginia, through eastern North Carolina, most of South Carolina, Georgia, and Alabama, northern Florida, Mississippi, and Louisiana, western Tennessee, and east Arkansas and Texas. Rural, heavily Negro in population ratios, increasingly poor—this flat belt gripped political power long after the cotton which had once made it powerful had fallen from the economic throne. The area in which racial prejudice and cultural backwardness are most pronounced still holds political sway, and, unhappily, provides the South with its typical spokesmen. It has been able to do so because of grossly inequitable representation in the state legislatures, concurred in by the moneyed interests of the region's cities, which have been grateful for the Black Belt's ingrained conservatism. Whenever, before and since the Civil War, there has been crisis, it is this area which has decided what the South will do; the other sections of the South—the prosperous, easy-going Piedmont, the mountains, the tolerant coastal fringe, the Catholic parishes of Louisiana, the upland valleys which never knew plantations—have been brought into line. That power of decision is today in jeopardy, and that is good news for the South, and, indeed, for the nation and the whole Atlantic community.

Old ways die hard. Because Southern society was organized on a racial division, all white men were in a sense comrades. Paradoxical strains of social and political equalitarianism wind through what is, nevertheless, an elitist structure. An occasional Huey Long has risen from the masses to combat the economic oppressors, but this has been the exception. William Faulkner's distrusted Snopses have largely displaced the old aristocracy, but by now several generations of them have held the reins and assumed the mantle of command, and their racial brothers tend to look upon them as the doers of the family business. There is among white Southerners a feeling of mutual inheritance, of a common sharing in the manners, the style, and the advantages of being a white man; and men have quite naturally grown accustomed to these and have come, also naturally, to regard them as values worthy of defense.

Learned persons have sometimes analyzed Southern racial attitudes and found at their roots dark and vital sexual motives. Perhaps this is correct. Certainly, the cult of woman exaltation was about all that Southern whites could possibly salvage from the chivalrous notions toppled by the Civil War, and to have retained and rebuilt upon that cult would have been a psychological expectancy. However this may be, white Southerners, living in what is a relatively advanced industrial society, have shown a remarkably intense resistance toward change in these racial relations which are their fraternal links. At the same time, there is almost no white Southerner who, by the time he emerges from adolescence, does not feel that he shares complicity in a social and moral decision which he can only hope is right, or, at worst, a venial wrong: yet one which he may very well suspect, or know, is neither. I have never met a white Southerner, not even the most determined of segregationists, who did not betray some moral uncertainty; and in that fact he differs and is set apart from the majority of his fellow Americans.

This is possibly a part of the reason why he will, often after the staunchest resistance, adapt so comfortably to new racial practices. Once the fight is decisively lost (the verdict has to be decisive), once the Negro has secured the right to vote, has gained admittance to the public library, has fought his way into a desegregated public school, has been permitted to sup at a lunch counter, the typical white Southerner will shrug his shoulders, resume his stride, and go on. He has, after all, shared a land with his black neighbors for a long while; he can manage well enough, even if the patterns change. There is now one fewer fight which history requires of him. He has done his ancestral duty. He is free of part of his load, he can relax a bit more. He has been annealed.

But, of course, neither can the typical white man give up without a fight, for that would not be dutiful to the past or to the intricate web of society which he, consciously or unconsciously, feels a need to sustain. So he will not be a leader in the reform of racial practice. What the Negro Southerner has won in the way of equality, therefore, he owes chiefly to himself and the federal courts. (Merely to credit the federal courts is too simple. They have been the instruments of the Constitution, and the racial reforms of recent years are a striking exhibition of the power of the concept of a fundamental law, undergirding and disciplining and guiding a nation.) By a series of judicial decisions, commencing in 1944, the right to vote is being secured. Decisions since 1948 have rendered housing segregation legally impossible (though social barriers are still high). A notable string of cases since 1938 has firmly established the right of Negroes to enter tax-supported colleges and universities. The epochal decision of 1954, in the case of *Brown v. Topeka*, declared the right of Negro children to a non-segregated education in the public schools.

It was the 1954 decision which produced the South's current rebellion. The South is again in siege, and the final days draw close. The environs have already been penetrated, the stores of the defenders have run low, the will to continue an unequal contest has dimmed. There is a widespread, and inexact, saying in America that the South lost the Civil War, but won the peace. In the manner of world politics, and with a similar regard for the costs, something like a cold war has been substituted these past seven years for armed combat. It will go on for a few years more; some of its bitterest, ugliest episodes, even more appalling than Little Rock, New Orleans, and Montgomery, probably lie ahead. But the South—the South, that is, of racial oppression and of enervating tradition—will lose again. And *that* South will not win the peace.

Leave for a time that assertion unjustified. What lies behind this upsurge of interest in and agitation of an old dilemma, to the point where racial relations and civil rights in the South have been America's principal domestic issue these late years? Consider first why the Negro people, who had ineffectually protested their lot for decades, suddenly became, after 1940, increasingly successful. Nothing is more impressively explanatory than the fact that the Negroes of America, in this generation, achieved a quantity of talent sufficient to lead and man a campaign. The arduous, persevering educational efforts, by churches, philanthropies, and public bodies had finally borne fruit. There were *enough* Negro lawyers and organizers and educated ministers and businessmen and teachers and students, enough talent finally to be heard. With but few and unimportant exceptions, these men have conducted the campaign for equal rights not only skillfully but with a clear intuition of responsibility. Especially among Southern Negroes, there has been comprehension that the objective was not to punish the South, but to make it acknowledge human rights and to do that in such a way as not to engender new or make permanent old bitterness.

But there is impatience as well as responsibility, and the tension between the two has so far been a creative one. The most spectacular display of the former is the student protest movement, begun February 1, 1960, in Greensboro, North Carolina, keyed to the device of the "sit-in," and spontaneously spread throughout the region. One student leader put it well: "We are not only entitled to service, but we want it." And that states concisely the meaning of the sit-ins. They represent a demand that white Southerners move now, without the compulsion of judicial decrees, to open communities for joint enjoyment and participation.

This came as quite a surprise to the South. The sit-ins were like the longbows of Crecy. That kind of an attack hadn't been expected, and it was disconcerting. It said to the white South, "Do this now, and do it of your own design, because we are all one community, for which you are, at the moment, the caretaker." Puzzled, yet dimly persuaded, the white South responded. And so, within a year, about one hundred cities and towns allowed integration at lunch counters and restaurants;

it was as surprising as the movement itself. The students brought a renewal of hope—for courage and willingness to suffer for right are always a cause for rekindling hopes. The white Southerners who in scores of places assented to the students' demands laid a basis for a new hope—that the white South might at last be ready to take its destiny in its own hands and, without compulsion of the federal government and its courts, move to build a true community of persons.

The sit-ins were an expression of impatience, but with almost unbelievably few lapses they have been conducted under canons of responsibility. A large part of the credit for this is owed to the example and teaching of the Reverend Dr. Martin Luther King, Jr. His commitment to the philosophy of Gandhi has magnetized the students toward the complementary poles of non-compromise and non-violence.

The Freedom Ride has been a more contrived and less indigenous protest than the earlier sit-ins. National public opinion is a phantom, eluding both measurement and intuition, and perhaps too much a vagrant to be ever addressed. One may, nevertheless, venture the guess that it is uneasy about the Ride. If so, the Negro campaign for equal rights and privileges has, for the first time in a long while, adopted a method disliked by national opinion.

Yet there is general approval of the Ride's objective, and there has been further advance toward a great accomplishment: i.e., the strengthening of communication between the races of the South. Friction and struggle have not, as so often has been alleged, broken down communication. The truth is that in recent years Negro Southerners, for the first time, have been communicating their true feelings and desires and beliefs and the white South has been hearing, and has been learning.

The student movement inevitably yielded proclamations of the advent of the "New Negro," who has, in fact, been announced almost as often, since the Civil War, as the "New South." There has also been great interest in the question of whether Negro Americans feel an identity with the emerging nationalism of Africa. A long and brilliant article by Harold R. Isaac in Phylon last year, "Five Writers and Their African Ancestors," suggests this answer: formally, yes; but essentially, only at the edges of their concern. Yet historians will surely want to probe and reflect on the coincidence of the surge forward in America and Africa, and the material and spiritual conditions of our time which drove both.

Among the material factors operative here, the expansion of the ranks of Negro talent has been already mentioned. Of equal, if not greater, importance have been the streaming exodus, since 1940, of Negro Southerners from the farm and their movement to cities of the South and North. This has not been an unalloyed blessing: it has thrust formerly stable, rural families into the solvent of city slums, involved Negroes in crime and juvenile delinquency to sickening degrees, and added to the already crushing problems of America's cities. But what was a cancer is now only a fever. The Black Belt has been a cancer eating into America's strength, draining it economically and morally, and frustrating its political policies through the terrific influence which inequitable representation has allowed this section to exert all the way to Congress. The practical interests of the men who hold power within it have been, usually, opposed to racial justice. There are certain ameliorative measures possible and therefore necessary; but there is little prospect of basic improvement in racial relations in the rural Black Belt until all the Negroes who are now marginal producers—and that includes most of them—move. In the cities, large and small, where the winds of impersonal democracy and commerce incline men and policies toward change and solutions rather than defense of status, fevers may run high, but can be, and usually are, cured in time.

1960 census reports reveal the vastness of the Negro migration. New York has the largest Negro population among American cities. Of the first fifteen cities, in numbers of Negroes, only three—Houston, Dallas, and New Orleans—are Southern, and they rank seventh, fourteenth, and fifteenth respectively. Final data are not yet available, but when they are they will show an extraordinary shift of Negroes from the farms of the South to cities, both Northern and Southern. In ratio of Negro to white the Southern cities are still highest, although the first in the South—Atlanta—is far lower than Washington, whose population is now 54 per cent Negro; Atlanta's is 38 per cent. State returns show that New York is now first in Negro residents, having been sixth in 1950. Five other states have more than 1,000,000 Negro inhabitants: they are, in order, Texas, Georgia, North Carolina, Louisiana, and

Illinois. The proportion of the nation's Negroes who live in the South declined from 81 per cent in 1910, to 60 per cent in 1950, to 52 per cent in 1960. Negroes have remained a fairly steady 10 to 11 per cent of the American population through several decades.

The white side of the Southern picture is equally fluid. For over a century—after about 1820—the South was not an integral part of the American economy. It is now. Still well below national levels of income and capital accumulation, it has nevertheless been incorporated within the general economy so that it prospers and it declines with the country as a whole. More pertinently, the income of urban whites in the South now approximates national levels. They are the servants of American industry and commerce, and they tend to think and conduct themselves like their fellow-servants in Northern and Western cities; indeed, they work for many of the same employers, for industrialization has been carried to the South principally through branch plants of national firms. Moreover, these plants have brought with them many non-Southerners, to fill managerial and technical positions. The commercial and industrial class, particularly those among it who wear white collars, has largely lost interest in defending the South's racial customs, has been the vanguard of every retreat, and comprises the people who said "yes" to the demands of the Negro students.

Yet there is more to the Southern struggle with itself than surrender to the ethos of commerce. The South's intellectuals have deserted her. Academic scholars have been mostly silent, and the universities politically sterile; at least, however, they have not given succor to tradition. Indeed, almost no one has, and can any institution live without intellectual defense? A distinguished group of editors, on the other hand, has not been silent: the idea of a free, responsible press has never had finer exemplars than men such as Ralph McGill, Lenoir Chambers, Harry Ashmore, Sylvan Meyer, A. M. Secrest,[1] and others like them who have cajoled and driven the South toward national unity. Nor has the Southern ministry been quiet, and as a consequence there has developed for the first time in the region's history a rift between pew and pulpit. It is altogether possible, however, that neither the editors nor the clergy have had an influence on Southern readiness to leave their hallowed cocoon equal to that of the immensely gifted Southern novelists of the period since 1920.

Auden said of Yeats that

> ... mad Ireland hurt you into poetry.
> Now Ireland has her madness and her weather still,
> For poetry makes nothing happen: it survives. ...

The Southern writers were also "hurt into" their poetry (for such it has typically been, even though in prose form), loving the South so tenaciously that they could write of nothing else, singing, as Auden also put it, "of human unsuccess / In a rapture of distress." They have probed the South's treasured myths, laid bare its agony of spirit and often meanness of motive, chastised its cultural timidity, and exposed its grotesqueries. They sobered for many of the South's brightest people the fun and pride of being a "Southerner," and cast abroad a picture of the South which was believed and which sensitive Southerners have ever since been wishful of changing. By surviving, their poetry *has* made things happen.

Change has been accompanied by, has been in part both cause and effect of, a decline in Southern political power. This has several facets. Presidents are chosen through a system of electoral votes that enhances the importance of populous states. With the single exception of Texas, the largest American states are characterized by close division of strength between Democrats and Republicans, and by growing Negro populations. The consequence is that the non-Southern Negro vote, which has the potential of tipping all of New York's or California's or Illinois' electoral votes one way or the other, has become more sought after in Presidential elections than Southern support. Presidents, therefore, beginning with Franklin D. Roosevelt, have been heavily committed to the strengthening of Negro rights and opportunities, though President Eisenhower successfully adhered in this as in other fields to his aversion for governmental action. President Kennedy, on the other hand, is using the powers of his office constructively. The order he has issued to enforce the ban against discrimination in employment by federal agencies and governmental contractors is thoroughly serious, and is being vigorously administered. His Attorney-General has placed the weight of the government in civil rights cases now before the courts. The President has realized both symbolic and practical effects by appointments of Negroes to high posts: those of Mr. Weaver as head of all housing agencies and of Mr. Wharton as Ambassador to Norway are especially noteworthy. (No Southerner has been nominated or elected President since 1848, unless Woodrow Wilson is counted. No Southerner has served since Johnson, and he was a Tennessean who had refused to secede. Of the ten men elected to the Presidency before 1848, six were from the South and a seventh had lived there until well into manhood.)

The bastion of Southern political influence has been Congress. Aided by the seniority system which determines committee chairmanships, Southerners have often monopolized the leadership of both Houses. Their power is still disproportionately great. It is not, however, what it once was; the passage in 1957 and again in 1960 of the first civil-rights laws in eighty years was evidence of the decline.

The federal government once before—from 1861 to 1877—had taken an active interest in the South's handling of its racial practices. That endeavor ended in confusion and ignoble compromise, and the result was that Negroes passed from slavery in a relatively rich society to unprotected peonage in a miserably poor one. The present period of national concern, buttressed by world-wide attention and prodded by alert Negro leaders, will not have the same ending.

The strength and adroitness of Southern resistance is measured by the mere eight hundred Negro children who, seven years after the Supreme Court's decision, are all that have been accepted into schools with white children in the South, outside of west Texas. But eight hundred is double what there were last year, and the corner has been turned. Georgia desegregates some schools in the city of Atlanta this September, and will evidently do so peacefully. Louisiana will, most likely, continue its tawdry show of racism, but an entering wedge has been driven in New Orleans. Only Alabama, Mississippi, and South Carolina will be left, and their day of reckoning comes closer. It is not likely to be a pleasant day either, for reckless, passionate men are in strong positions in all three states. The sit-ins have produced some desegregation of eating places in every state except these three and Louisiana.

The old tether has been snapped. No longer does the Black Belt control the rest of the South. The Black Belt has been seceded from.

The South has been, like Spain, Ireland, or southern Italy, one of the cultural anomalies of the Atlantic community. Pulled forward by Negroes, including its own, and pushed along by the federal government and national opinion, the South is about to take on a new character. Not yet for a while, however, will it disappear as a culture. There is here too much history, too flavorsome a life, too ingrained a style. But if the South does in time disappear and blend itself indistinguishably with the larger nation, it has still ahead an opportunity that it can fulfill better than any place or people anywhere.

I believe that the South will, out of its travail and sadness and requited passion, give the world its first grand example of two races of men living together in equality and with mutual respect. The South's heroic age is with us now.

2

Civil Rights and Civil Duties

1962

This October 28, 1962, speech made in New York seems almost innocent in its non-awareness of the awful events that lay ahead. The rebellion at the University of Mississippi and hard struggles at Albany, Georgia, had already happened, and I do not know why I did not mention them—I had been close to the Albany ones and to everything in Mississippi. But Dallas still did lie ahead, and after it all innocence evaporated.

But the idealism that infused this speech did not. The civil rights movement, so long as it truly remained a movement, never gave that up. Nor, and this was just as important, did it surrender its realism. It never ceased knowing and acting on the knowledge that the conditions of the southern poor were uncivilized and that southern politics was, too, and vile at that. Decades later, it still inclines that way, and the poor still suffer. Much of this speech seems to me, despite its omissions, still about right. But its optimism that deep change in southern political leadership lay ahead does not. I see no reason to change my 1962 assertion that the South's politicians have been wrong every time in their regional leadership. Nor, on the other hand, my sense of there being throughout the world an essential "yearning" for unity.

I feel sure that the planners of this meeting had no expectation that it would occur at such a time as this. The years of the cold war have taught each of us an ability to live, in some way or another, with constant tension. Not before this last week, however, have we been so close to what has been dreaded for so long.

I think we cannot but wonder what effects war, or an intensification of the cold war, would have on the struggle for civil rights with which we are engaged. I shall not try any public speculation about that, except to note that there would undoubtedly be a loss, in some degree, of public and governmental interest. There is a sort of tragic irony in the reflection that both of the last two world wars followed and interrupted periods of great social reform in the United States. Since the close of World War II we have been in another such period, this one having to do with reform of human relations. These are bitter coincidences to contemplate.

But today also in Rome an inspiring event is unfolding, as the ecumenical conference which that good man, Pope John, has summoned continues its deliberations. We live in a fractured world today, but one which seems to have within it a throbbing impulse, an essential yearning, for unity. We see it everywhere. The Protestant denominations take small, hesitant steps toward unification. Nations cling to the U.N. Western Europe moves steadily toward common institutions. Sectionalism in our country yields to national values. And everywhere, men are letting fall the blinders of their souls, and are seeing with new clarity and concern the lives of other men. The popularity of slogans reveal much about what people really believe and wish. That line of John Donne's—"No man is an island"—has been quoted so many countless times that it has by now become a slogan, and one that reveals our deepest hopes.

I believe that the civil rights movement is an outcome of the soul yearning that has made the line, "No man is an island," a living, breathing, popular prayer. When we ask ourselves why there has been, since 1944, a great surge forward in civil rights we can give many answers—economic, political, educational. But underlying all has been, I think, a newfound, small, still voice within us that says "yes" to unity, "no" to division, that says "yes" to brotherhood, "no" to separation and segregation.

It is likely that nearly all persons reached by these words are convinced that segregation is a moral evil. We believe that segregation is iniquitous and unjust, and we are confident that our belief is right. Although knowing very little theology, I have the impression that there is general agreement among well nigh all religions that there is no sin greater than that of pride. Do we run the risk of falling into the sin of pride through our conviction that our moral judgment about racial relations is the right one, and that of the traditional South is wrong and evil? Are the righteous as well as the wicked prone to pridefulness?

These are, I think, not vain questions, but timely and practical ones. During the next few years, we shall be needing all the moral stamina we can summon. We shall need it not only for our racial and personal problems, but because these will be occurring against the backdrop of a chaotic, frightening, and scared world. Because of the democratic advances made since 1944, when the white primary was outlawed and the civil rights momentum began, Negro and liberal white men and women have and will have ever-increasing political influence. Unless we can school ourselves to accept this influence and power calmly and unpretentiously, ours will be a sorry triumph.

For, as I understand it, at the heart of the civil rights movement is a repugnance against the over-use of power. But even deeper than this there is a commitment within the civil rights movement, at its best, in favor of the belief that a good society is a society of people linked together through gentleness of spirit. And, even though most workers for civil rights whom I know are people of realism, who expect no Utopias now or ever, they are, I believe, people who are devoted to "that city laid up in heaven" made up of gentle people. And in that city they try to live. Indeed, the very term civil rights resembles and has a common root with that other word, "civility," which describes the manner in which civilized men and women live with each other. So when we work for civil rights we are really working for the civilized behavior of people toward each other; we are working for civility.

We are, then, on trial. We are, through the magnificent leadership of the NAACP, its Legal Defense and Education Fund, the Rev. Martin Luther King, Jr., and hundreds of adult and youth crusaders all over the South, winning the campaign for civil rights. There are ahead some very rough days. But as certain as these are, victory is equally certain. And we are on trial. We shall have to prove that we have no desire to punish those who opposed us. We shall have to prove that, having secured the civil rights of Negro Americans, we now are ready to go about the rest of the Lord's work.

Here in this luxurious hotel that civility I spoke of a moment ago is everywhere. In this setting we may find it easy to forget that the fundamental issues have to do with persons who never come to this hotel or any place like it. The hardest wrought issues of civil rights concern those whom an earlier and more romantic generation would have called the down-trodden masses. If you want to find these people you will have to go into the vile tenements of Harlem. Or into a lifeless county of rural Mississippi where white men with worn-out wives and worn-out land and too many children drag themselves through a bewitching southern climate with nothing really important to do and no hope of finding anything to do which will give their lives self-respect. Or you will have to look in some alley of a southern city or town, heavy with the oppressive yet somehow friendly odor of frying catfish, where Negro children, too numerous to count easily, are the only spots of brightness in the human scene. Or you will have to look in the camps of the migrant workers, who are truly America's forgotten people, as they make their way up and down the eastern seaboard and into the gardens of California and into the broad lands of the Midwest. America likes to call itself a middle class country. If it were wholly a middle class country, there would be, I suspect, as much fetid prejudice of all kinds as we have today and perhaps even more. But I venture to believe that we would not have the problems which currently make the struggle for civil rights so grim. It is the disadvantaged tenth of American people, both white and Negro, who give the tense seriousness to racial relations. Asking these people to acknowledge the civil rights of others or to accept and exercise the rights which are theirs under the American constitution, is like asking people on whom a whole society stomps to behave with civility. These people are outcasts of civilization.

Consequently they act as such. Why should we, after all, be surprised if a handful of semi-illiterate white men in an impoverished county, having spent what little change they have on a bottle of booze, and having nothing else to do or even to wish for, go off and burn a Negro church? Why should we be surprised if, despite all the efforts of Negro community organizations, families confined to a vermin-infested ghetto do not send off to the public schools children who are models of behavior and intellectual curiosity?

We have millions of people in America for whom the American standard of living, the American way of life, the affluent society are but the emptiest of phrases. These people include Negroes, Puerto Ricans, Mexicans, white folk of the rural South, and others as well. I believe that the next great task of our nation should and will be a massive effort to reclaim this social wreckage. At the present, a very large proportion of this bottom tenth of the population is Negro.

Well, of course, the white supremacists (who live, incidentally, both in the North and South) are right about one thing. Negroes are often poor, often have high crime rates, often have low educational records, often display personal and family irresponsibility, *simply because they are Negroes*. And that this should be a fact is a sin of the white race as enormous and as hideous as other sins of the white race, such as Hitler's cremations and Stalin's starvation of the peasants. After having hammered at the Negro consciousness and vitality by 300 years of slavery, brutality, discrimination, and segregation, some of us seem now perplexed to discover that many Negroes do not behave well. It is altogether proper to be disturbed on account of this, and to deliver a rebuke. But let's deliver it at the right door.

The behavior standards of many Negroes, just as the behavior standards of white mobsters of the South, are a rebuke against the whole nation. We sowed, and we reap. And we will not reap a good grain, unless we cultivate with care and loving attention. No minority can lift itself out of poverty by its own bootstraps, unless, like the Jews or the Orientals, it is a people with its own religion, its own communal exclusiveness, its own traditions and history, and its own pride. If you want Negroes to lift themselves by their own bootstraps, then make way for the Black Muslims. Perhaps in a century or two they could do it. But if you don't want Black Muslims, if you don't want to wait centuries, then you and the rest of America must assume responsibility for curing the disease which America caused. We need to stop talking about the "Negro problem," and to start talking and thinking and acting about the nation's moral *and* economic *and* political necessity for rescuing the millions whom we have cut adrift and who now hang like a ball and chain about the necks of the rest of us.

Moreover, we need to stop talking about the "Negro problem" if for no other reason than common courtesy and good manners. Down South, one of the traditional roles of the Negro house servant was to make the white children of the house mind their manners. I hope my good friend Henry Moon, of the NAACP, will not object if I thank him, because he, wearily but patiently, took time out recently to resume this ancient function of his race, by writing a letter to a certain magazine, trying to teach the white folks once again how to mind their manners.[1]

Some are so disturbed by the civic performance of many Negroes that they urge that we shift our main campaign now away from civil rights and toward the improvement of Negro habits, character, and ambitions. We have to remember that for a long, long time, under the guidance of Booker T. Washington and white philanthropists, a great effort was made on behalf of the improvement of Negroes, on the premise that this was the way to gain admittance to the rights and dignities of the white man's free society. Much good resulted from these efforts, and we are all today in the debt of those people who during the late 19th and early 20th centuries worked so hard and in such loneliness. What a huge debt we owe, for example, to those few who worked even better than they knew how to lay the beginnings of the Negro colleges and universities which are in fact the wellsprings of today's civil rights movement and of the proud Negro leadership which inspires and directs it.

But we have to admit also that this approach did not work in two important particulars: one was that no matter how much he improved himself the Negro was *not* admitted to the white man's free society. And secondly, we found out that there were sharp limitations on how much Negroes could improve themselves unless they had the rights of free men.

We learned, if we had our senses about us, that in a democracy and in a free enterprise economy only the people who have civil rights can obtain the advantages which we all want and require. Civil rights precede civic improvement; the opposite is not the case.

And there is a long way yet to go before the civil rights of Americans are made secure. There are fields such as housing and white collar employment and family relationships which have hardly yet been scratched. I am one of those optimistic, perhaps naive, Southerners who believe that we can in the South do a lot better with an old challenge than have our brothers to the North. White Southerners have always claimed to know "their" Negroes, and Negro Southerners have claimed to know "their" white folks, and there has been a good bit of self deception and blarney in both claims but also enough truth to give us in the South the groundwork for building decent towns and neighborhoods and churches, once the civil rights war is over and won. For in some valuable measure we Negroes and whites of the South do know each other, are not strangers, have shared a regional consciousness, have been poor together, have revealed our meanness and have got a lot of the enormous supply of it out of our systems. We have no secrets from each other. We know each other's sinfulness and weakness and mulishness. There is a tolerance and a kind of affection, and when we get beneath the rancor and the passion—and the hate—we shall have something solid to build on.

We shall have in the South some old myths to lay to rest. For example, one of the distinctive traits of the South has been the trust, almost the veneration, we have given our leaders. We followed and believed in Mr. Jefferson, and Calhoun, and Jefferson Davis, and Lee, and the Redeemers, and Carter Glass, and James Byrnes, and Richard Russell. Mention these names to many Southerners and you set their spines atingle.

Perhaps we of the South will never get over our immaturity until we confront a plain fact which generations of Southerners have conspired together in avoiding. The fact is this: our politicians have been wrong every time in their regional leadership. At every great crisis in southern history our political leaders did the wrong thing, wrong for the nation, and wrong for the South. No people has ever had less cause to be grateful to its statesmen than we of the South.

A new leadership is emerging. Because the record behind us is so incredibly poor, we have to ask, "Will the new be better?" Will Negroes and liberal whites know how to lead, as their day comes? Are we a region capable of self-government?

Consequently, the happiest thing I have to report to you is that the desegregation controversy is bringing peace, not bitterness, relaxation, not continued tension, to the South. You may be amazed to hear this; those who know and love the South would not be. As my friend and boss, John Wheeler of Durham, N. C., likes to say, Southerners are the most adaptable people in the world. Once the crisis has passed, once a battle for civil rights has been fought and decisively won, your typical white Southerner relaxes, accepts it, feels better about the whole thing, and goes on about his business. I believe I can report to you that Atlanta and Richmond and Nashville and Greensboro and many other localities of the South are happier cities today than they have ever been. And the explanation is simple: they are freeing themselves from an ancient, huge, oppressive problem.

If I give you a report of good tidings, I must in fairness add a warning. The civil rights movement has now penetrated the Deep South, even into the rural Black Belt. We shall have, and I say this with all the gravity I can command, some of the worst, if not the very worst, conflicts that we have ever encountered.

But the main tide is running clear and strong, and it will be hastened along. There will be, for example, over the next two years unprecedented resources and energies put into voter registration campaigns throughout the South. Those who are working in this campaign are not merely trying to register Negroes; they are working as the country's servants, in behalf of the extension and perfection of democracy. Through their efforts, the control of southern politics, which has extended all the way from county courthouse to Congress, and which affects even our foreign policies, is being broken.

One of the truly notable characteristics of Negro Americans has been that, when they have asked for relief from racial injustices, they have almost invariably given three justifications for their demands. First and second, they have said we want justice and we are entitled to it. But they always add a third reason. Sometimes they may say the economic welfare of the country requires that discrimination be ended; sometimes it may be that democracy requires it; sometimes, that God requires it. To put it in other words, Negroes relate their campaign for civil rights to other goals. They see racial justice as not only an end in itself, but a necessary means to other ends: democracy, the American Dream, the Judeo-Christian truths. This habit of mind is a very wonderful thing. We white people can only be humbly thankful for it. That Negroes should consistently join their cause to some other, and often higher, end is a revelation of magnificent spirits and mind.

Now we must all learn that spirit. We need to learn that free men have civil duties. That among these civil duties are the obligations to secure and exercise our own rights; to demand and defend rights for others; to exercise our rights and fulfill our duties because we acknowledge service to causes higher than our own self-interest; to deserve the respect of all men; and to grant our respect to each of our human brothers.

3

The Changing Mind of the South: The Exposed Nerve

1964

This was the lead essay in the Southern Political Science Association's 1964 symposium on the South. Early pages of it were given over to such questions as to the essence of the South and Southernness, and few seem to care about that anymore, so in that regard this may be the most dated essay in this present book. Some of its questions will have to be answered, if at all, by its readers; for example, is it still worthwhile to call oneself a Southerner?

But the South that the essay perceived as emerging is unlike any that followed the Civil War. It is a South throwing itself into the contest for leadership of the national character. Some of my prophecies are plainly wrong, for example, that the "American consensus of our latter days would reject what Mississippi represents." It has, instead, come close especially during Republican ascendancies to embracing it, even as the state itself is moving away from it in some positive ways, so close, in fact, that I have to doubt my statement toward the end of section IV that neutrality between competing economic interests is "commonplace" in our national politics.

But other prophecies, most notably the one with which the piece concludes, have proved sadly correct.

I

I premise that there has been such a thing as a southern folk, clearly if not definably more a single people than any other Americans, composed of two grades of persons, both of whom have been truly part of the same folk, and yet one of whom, the Negro Southerners, because they were ruled by the other did not sense and hallow as did the whites their folk integrity and their distinctness from the rest of the nation. And because white Southerners have consciously known that they were set apart, they have struggled to define themselves, have striven for self-identity, and with every Cash or Percy—or Faulkner—asking "Who am I?" have moved nearer the point which comes in every self-examination, where discovery means either release or reunion.

Who is there who is not tired of this search, who would not rather give it up before he has to choose between release, and rejection, or recoil into the mind of the South, who would rather not stop short in self-discovery and become what history makes of him? And indeed, there has been a re-directing of the South's self-study. The intellectual and artistic concern is changing, has changed, from a deep, self-combative hoeing and chopping of souls and history and eternity, and toward commitment to the active issues of the day. The dark, Faulknerian problems recede.

The classic interpreters of the South began with the conviction that there was a "South" and a "Southerner," and they hunted for definitions. Because the interpreters were themselves Southerners, dredging their prey up through their memories and revealing it as a Protean substance, their definitions were never abstract, and they never tired of examining countless aspects. Nor did they, however, ever yield the belief that something constant and essential lay under the aspects. The Southerner was to be known as a being, and not an active one at that. Only the public figures of the South defined themselves in activity, and the interpreters tended to be less interested in them than in regarding the South's election of them as another aspect of the essential being which needed to be pondered. The essential Southerner acted occasionally, savagely and without premeditation, and this proclivity of his was another aspect to be explained. But except for this, the Southerner "was"; he did not, since the Civil War, "do."

Our preoccupation today is with how Southerners do and will act. For this is a time of testing. We are re-learning an old truth, which historians have nearly always known and social scientists have frequently forgotten, that men reveal themselves more accurately through their action than through their established feelings, opinions, and beliefs.

Another change has occurred as well. Cash, writing as late as 1941, was not really much attentive to Negro Southerners, and Percy, writing also in 1941, could say that he was "usually in a condition of amazed exultation over the excellent state of race relations in the South." James Agee, almost the quintessential New Dealer, took only an occasional and not seriously interested glance at the Negro neighbors of his white Alabama sharecroppers. Of the classic writers, only Lillian Smith had the greatness to wrestle with what the others saw, but passed by, and that was the centrality of race to the southern self-consciousness.[1]

In fact, not until the sit-in movement began in Greensboro in 1960 did the "mind" of Negroes become of conscious interest to white Southerners, in the sense that an active awareness began that the southern consensus had to include Negro values and desires. Even in the titanic controversies after 1954, the actors—those who were conspicuously making history—were almost always white: Senator Byrd, Governor Faubus, and the other captains of massive resistance. Negroes appeared only as a shadowy mass, from whom now and then emerged an impersonal lawyer or a poker-faced schoolchild walking through white faces lit with expression. The state of North Carolina might well put one of its historical markers at that dime store in Greensboro: here is where, after more than three centuries, the white and the Negro South were finally met.

In result, they have learned to know each other better. One Negro civil rights leader remarked to me that southern racial relations in the past had been like an unfaithful marriage, which could be preserved only by the two parties not speaking the truth to each other. Negro Southerners are today speaking the truth to their white neighbors. If white Southerners can learn to live with this truth, the marriage can be continued, and may even become a fruitful one. Still today, no Southerners are more bred to the essence of the region's distinctive history, manners, and outlook than are the Negroes. If Dixie is not yet ready for its epitaph, it will be only because Negroes, freed of illegitimacy, may give it new life.

For earlier white Southerners, even for those as late as Cash, a decision about racial policies was not socially crucial. Men had different opinions and beliefs, but these were like other personal preferences, or even convictions, that were tolerable by the folk. Southern racial relations were like Hinduism, able to absorb and contain many changes and interests and ideas. The advent of industrialization, the steady immigration of non-Southerners, the growth of learning, the magnification of cities—all had come and had modified the old patterns and would surely in time overthrow them. But the endurance—what a Southerner might call the "cussedness"—of the old ways was remarkable.

But now this changes, and I know no better way to illustrate the change at its profoundest—though infrequently perceived—level than by contrasting Faulkner with that present-day southern writer who, in surface aspects, is most like him. The genius of Faulkner was such that he was able to suffuse his characters in life and individuality even though, in fact, they were little more than marionettes. They were held in the hand of God, but that hand which controlled them kept them in ceaseless confrontation with their home, i.e., with southern history, and in it they defined themselves. Miss Flannery O'Connor's characters are also marionettes and also in the grasp of God. They are Southerners too, but this is only an artist's detail. They could be anyone, they are caught directly, as simple individuals, in the human predicament, and they act directly to meet it, not, as Faulkner's characters always did, as Southerners, but as mere people.

Fundamentally, this is where Southerners find themselves today, forced to act directly without validating their acts against their history, much of which is sinking fast underneath them. Another southern writer, Allen Tate, in his novel *The Fathers*, depicts the deep psychological hurt felt by conservative Virginians in 1860–1861 when pressures from the cotton states and from the North were mysteriously pushing Virginia into severance from the government in Washington, of which over the years since 1787 they had come to feel as proprietors. Something similar is happening today over the South, as men see institutions which they had thought were theirs (e.g., the churches, the town school), relationships which they had thought secure (e.g., mistress and maid), begin to take on new shape and purpose.

All this has meant that, for today's white Southerner, an explicit rationalizing of his views about race has become the most urgent of his intellectual and spiritual tasks, and that he has had to achieve it on his own, or with new referents. He has had to attune himself, harmoniously or discordantly, to the authoritative words and practices of institutions from outside his region, such as the federal government, national church bodies, national media, and even—in fact—Wall Street. Perhaps still a man living in a remote Black Belt county untouched as yet by racial controversy may be as unengaged as nearly all of us were but a few years past. But I suspect that no white man living now in a Danville or an Albany or a Birmingham can support himself either by mores or by Faulknerian brooding. For the strong segregationist, the mores will appear too mild when the protest comes; for nearly all men, the brooding will seem irrelevant.

It is astonishing how often a southern white liberal can date his acceptance of racial equality at some specific episode in his life, much as did the ex-Communists in *The God That Failed*[2] tend to date their break with Communism with a decisive, illuminating event. It is even more notable that almost every liberal can (and often does) recount the history of his changing attitudes. This sort of keen self-awareness occurs only with those life problems deeply and genuinely felt. Nevertheless, in accepting racial equality, the southern liberal does not typically reject the South. In Turgenev's *Fathers and Sons*, when Bazarov's tolerance of an older conservative is asked—"you must take into account his upbringing as well as the times in which he lived the best part of his life"—Bazarov exclaims: "His upbringing: Every man should educate himself. . . . As to the times, why should I depend upon them: Much better they should depend on me. No, brother, all that is just loose thinking, there's nothing solid behind it!" To a Southerner, if to no one else, this is questionable doctrine, because inadequate tolerance; and rightly or wrongly, the key word of southern liberalism has been "tolerance."

Southern liberalism deserves more serious study than it has had. What, in this context, is worth remarking is the long sustained refusal of southern liberals to repudiate the South, and this is one side of the tolerance which they have elevated above all other social virtues. Few liberals have acted out their beliefs. They do not try to enter their children in Negro schools, do not usually refuse to eat in segregated restaurants or worship in segregated churches, do not spontaneously and widely mingle socially with their Negro peers. This is not well described as either hypocrisy or timidity. It is something a good bit more basic. The general conformity of the liberal to social practices which he opposes is a mark of his dogged refusal to alienate himself from southern society. He has counted himself a Southerner, with an obligation to respect the community and, so far as possible, to keep it whole. He often will, in fact, contend (and not only from polemical motives) that he—and not the defenders of segregation—represents the core of southern traditions, and he will sometimes appeal to other values acknowledged to be "southern," such as "courage," or "manners" or "individuality," against the less venerable practice of segregation. The tenacity with which liberals hold to southern culture, while endeavoring to reform it, is a quality which cannot be measured, but it would seem at least as intense as the somewhat comparable spirit of the Benthamites and later Labourites in England; they too insisted on behaving as Englishmen as they went about changing the country.

On the whole, this attitude of respect toward the community is not alien to a great many of the Negro leaders. And on the whole, this shared attitude presents the only real possibility, for those of us who want one, of preserving the South as a cultural organism, and not merely as a cultivated, but mummified, memory, analogous to New England. It is not a very strong possibility, though the relative poverty of the region may help along its chances: poverty is a strong folk-tie. I may be wrong and shortly proved so, but I see the white South today, outside the Black Belt but even there in some measure, as disposed, though often reluctantly, to accept more and more racial integration, but wanting also to keep the community much as it has been. I see Negro Southerners wanting equality desperately and angrily, but disposed to keep the community much as it has been, if they are admitted to it.

The South that Cash sought to track down was the white South, and, assuming that Cash found what he sought, it was unprepared for 1954. That South is still here. But because, being what it was and is, it stayed distant from the black South, called itself and itself only "the South," it has become an inert thing, a mere environment. Within this environment and against it, the southern leaders of today—the Negroes— act. It is the antithesis of motion against matter, and unless it can be cured there is not even a meager chance that the South will persevere. The white South is become an object, and only subjects can, even in a Faulknerian sense, endure.

II

Myrdal remarked that, "The intellectual energy spent on the Negro problem in America should, if concentrated in a single direction, have moved mountains."[3] In truth, almost the profoundest thing one can say about southern race relations is that it is an old problem, toughened and complicated and made wondrously intricate by age, which has confused its diagnosis, rendered uncertain its treatment, and obscured its prognosis. Ancient as it is, it has had changing definitions, and these have, in the past, been determined by the interests and policies of white people. As Myrdal put it,

> It is thus the white majority group that naturally determines the Negro's "place." All our attempts to reach scientific explanations of why the Negroes are what they are and why they live as they do have regularly led to determinants on the white side of the race line. In the practical and political struggles of effecting changes, the views and attitudes of the white Americans are likewise strategic. The Negro's entire life, and, consequently, also his opinions on the Negro problem, are, in the main, to be considered as secondary reactions to more primary pressures from the side of the dominant white majority.[4]

This analysis was undeniably correct as an interpretation of the pre-1945 period; it is no longer so. Beginning about the close of World War II, the power to determine the Negro's "place" began to shade off from white control. Today, the Negro grip on the levers of social change is secure, and much more firm than the remnants of white direction.

The race relations policy of the southern white leadership from 1619 until Reconstruction, and from about 1890 until the 1940's, was governed by the objective, *How to get the maximum satisfaction from the Negro population.* The policy was pursued in economic, political, and social relationships, frequently with unsuccess. This fairly unanimously held single policy has, in the years since the 40's, been both losing adherents and singleness of application; the growth of Negro votes combined with pressures from Washington are forcing on our public life policies markedly more progressive than those which still dominate our churches and other more or less privately determined activities. Perhaps only in Mississippi today is there near unanimity about racial policy. But it is not the old policy of maximum satisfaction. Instead, it is, *How to maintain white control of the institutions of society*. At least, Negroes are not regarded as instruments and tools, but as antagonists. That, in itself, is a higher status.

If initiative has passed from the white majority to the Negro minority, the principal cause has been the success of Negroes in achieving a new and more stable self-knowledge. The dilemma—intellectual, emotional, political—of the Negro, especially the Negro male, has always been the problem of identity.[5] A man's valuation of himself is derived and sustained by his reading of other people's assessment of him, and at all times in a person's life there are some "other people" whom he regards as the most authoritative assessors. Because of history and color, Negroes for centuries got maddeningly confusing reports whenever they inquired of their society, "Who am I?"

With some notable variations, they adopted the social values and standards of the dominant white society. For generations, Negro Southerners had no sustained insight into white society beyond their own neighborhood, and they consequently shaped their self-portrait through the terms of local opinion. The past three or four decades have been a time, even for rural Negroes, of awareness of a larger universe of values and authoritative opinions, and increasingly they have tended to disregard local definitions in preference for more favorable nation-wide and world-wide judgments of their worth. But even in the old days, the answer to their question, "Who am I?", was far from clear. The Christianity they had been taught affirmed some things so surely that not even the utmost ingenuity of white pastoral apologists could altogether obscure them. The grand generalities of American democracy seeped into their consciousness. Their white neighbors behaved toward them with contradictory manners, producing what was (and, to a large extent, still is) surely one of the most weirdly implausible patterns of human relations ever observed. And always, Negroes were accompanied by a few stereotypes which sprang easily into the minds of white persons, even those a Negro might regard as friends, and displaced the actual Negro person they knew—or thought they knew.

The stereotypes were and are the damning judgments of white society on Negro identity. What is happening today is that Negroes are disowning the stereotypes, the white man's creations, are refusing any longer to acknowledge themselves to *be* what the white man said they were. White Southerners are confronted with a blunt demand from the Negro that he be accepted on his terms: *and this is the crucial problem of race relations today.* For years, whites have decreed that Negroes must think of themselves as the whites thought of them. Negroes now are insisting that the white majority revise its opinion of them in accord with their own, newly fashioned self-conception.

Negroes found that in the same European-American culture which had relegated them to inferiority, white supremacy had become a strand of that culture which "tends to wear away protective strata, to break down its own defenses, to disperse the garrisons of its entrenchment." The words are Schumpeter's,[6] and taken from a context which, though not analogous, is suggestive. Some other words of his are exactly applicable to contemporary Negro agitation: "Secular improvement that is taken for granted and coupled with individual insecurity that is acutely resented is of course the best recipe for breeding social unrest."[7] A concatenation of economic and educational factors, supported haphazardly and minimally by politics, produced the secular improvement; another array of political, emotional, and social circumstances caused and kept strong the individual insecurity. The social unrest is a direct outcome of the combination, and is given its specific form and intensity through the re-infusion of ideas and values into American culture by a constantly growing number of educated Negroes who have derived these ideas and values from the cultural property of western white peoples, the terms of whose inheritance require them to admit nonwhites with whom they come into regular communication to equal shares in the property.

III

Lincoln began his Gettysburg Address by recalling that "fourscore and seven years ago" there had been brought forth "a new nation conceived in liberty and dedicated to the proposition that all men are created equal." If, in this centennial year of the Emancipation Proclamation, of Gettysburg and Vicksburg, we look back four score and seven years, we confront a less happy and auspicious event: 1876, the year when Hayes defeated Tilden, or Tilden defeated Hayes, whichever it was. Hayes became President through the Compromise of 1877, and for the next 70 years or so the white South was left alone by the nation in its policies and in its relationships toward Negro citizens.

The Civil War had freed the slaves and preserved the union. It had, besides, put on two Amendments to the Constitution—the 14th and 15th—which in the years after 1876 would be, as to Negroes, well nigh meaningless: four generations of Negro and white Southerners would come and go and live without acknowledging that Negroes could and should vote, or that laws should give them equal protection. The Civil War, moreover, left all these people in a ravished region, where men would get used to desperate poverty. The War and its aftermath made the South feel its spiritual and cultural separation from the rest of the nation more keenly even than before.

Then, earlier, and now, we have defined "the South" by its differences from the rest.

Southerners and non-Southerners have been, in fact, much alike. White men everywhere ruled, and Negroes were subservient, and treated as inferiors. Society belonged—and still largely does—to the white man. Protestants ruled, dominating the economic and cultural and political life of the nation. Society placed a high sentimental value on farm or small-town culture and people, and long after the bulk of our population moved into cities the rural districts kept political power. And North and South, East and West, we all believed that any man who worked hard could get ahead.

These common qualities of American life, native both to the South and the non-South, are dissolving. And the present crisis in the South, which became acute in 1954, does not result from traditional differences from the nation; it results instead from the dissolution of things which have in the past united us.

Six landmark dates conveniently illustrate the changes. Although they affect the whole nation they are a special challenge to the South. Somebody—Arthur Koestler, I think—once spoke of the Jews as humanity's exposed nerve, feeling first and most sharply all the troubles and pains. Sometimes one feels that the South is America's exposed nerve, and that issues which are national in scope are most intense, or at least most apparent, here.

There was 1944, and *Smith v. Allwright*, and the ensuing erosion of the white monopoly of power to make political decisions. There was 1954, and *Brown v. Topeka*, which in its deeper import signified that the civic institutions of American society could no longer be operated as if they were the property of one race, and which, in its application since the New Rochelle case,[8] has upset the North as well as the South. There was 1960, and confirmation that non-Protestants have a share in the power to make the country's highest decisions. There was 1962, and *Baker v. Carr*, and the consequent remarkably fast crumbling of the rural fortress of political power.

There was 1940, the last year before our entry into World War II, the last year of a peace-time economy. After seven years of prodigious effort by the New Deal, unemployment in the United States was 14.6% of the working force. We went into the war and unemployment virtually ceased. We came out of the war and unemployment stayed low while the country was busily engaged in converting to peace-time needs. We had a recession in 1948, and the next year unemployment shot up to 5.9%. We went into the Korean fighting, and again unemployment declined. We had another recession in 1954, and unemployment was up again. We had yet another recession in 1958, and this time unemployment really rose—to 6.8% of the working force of this country. After each recession, recovery was slower. There has been little improvement since, and President Kennedy in March 1963, called unemployment our "number 1 economic problem," and reported that it was still about 6%; the rate for August 1963 was a seasonal 5.5%. Many economists believe that the government's way of computing unemployment seriously minimizes its extent.[9]

Neither the policies of Republican nor Democratic administrations have, as yet, been able to lick this problem. Unemployment is high despite the boosting of the economy with huge expenditures for armaments and for space exploration; without those would we be back to the 14.6% unemployed of 1940?

Here we meet a tragic irony; as has happened in the past, Negroes seem to be the victims not only of discrimination, but of impersonal history. After the first World War the country severely restricted the flow of immigrants from abroad. Up to then, American industry had grown by drawing on a boundless labor supply of European immigrants. With immigration drastically cut, industry met its need for new labor by drawing from the farms of America, including those of the South. Beyond this last large supply of white manpower, waited in economic succession the Negro. The tragic irony is that when his turn is come, the job market is declining. This is occurring in manufacturing and mining, chiefly, and these are fields which have been a gateway for new entrants into the free competition for economic advancement. No one seriously can continue to believe that America is for everyone now a land of opportunity where any man, unaided, can get ahead by dint of his own hard work. Some five to seven per cent or more of those people who want to work, find that there are no jobs, even though there is general prosperity in the country, and for the Negro the unemployment rate is about double that for whites.[10]

And, finally, there was 1947, when Mr. Truman appointed the President's Committee on Civil Rights, and later espoused its recommendations, even at the cost of a party split at the Democratic convention of 1948. No political act since the Compromise of 1877 has so profoundly influenced race relations; in a sense, it was the repeal of 1877. Among the consequences were (a) a shift of emphasis from Negro "uplift"—essentially a paternalistic approach—to civil rights, i.e., the achievement of more than nominal citizenship; (b) a renewal of the fateful rupture between South and non-South; and (c) the ensuing complications for economic and social reform by statute, so that, since 1948, law-making for domestic problems has fallen into desuetude.[11]

These six landmarks suggest, if I am not mistaken, that we shall have much more democracy in the United States. The price of that will be the ending of certain old ways and traditions. Groups who have led and controlled the country from its earliest days will have to accept a lessening of their influence. And if the South had trouble joining the old union—which, like it, was white, Protestant, and rural in its outlook and leadership—can it join this new union? The South was separated from the basically similar non-South of yesterday by a sharp enough cleavage; the new division would be a gulf.

To put it differently, the policies which Mississippi represents would not merely perpetuate North-South differences. The longer these policies are pursued, the greater becomes the alienation of Mississippi and the Black Belt generally from the American consensus. Just by standing pat, residents of these places will become strangers in their own land, because the nation as a whole is moving farther and farther from them.

IV

Over the years, Negro Southerners tried various methods of effecting change. They occasionally resorted to violence in the slave revolts of the ante-bellum period. During Reconstruction they sought the power of office. In Populist days they experimented—to their sorrow—with an electoral alliance with small farmers and mechanics. They tried the Booker T. Washington regimen of self-improvement, in the expectation that they would be accepted when their uplift was completed. They left the South, for the uncertain and often unrewarding North and West.

Finally—and with really their only success—they converted the political issue of equality into the Constitutional issue of equal rights. The "direct-action" movement has been a new force, and one of tremendous effect. It has produced results and it has unleashed and directed energies. Yet even its appeal has been to values thought to be in or implied by the Constitution, and the safety and success of the movement have been protected throughout by the procedural guarantees of the Constitution. The reform of the Negro question in the United States has been a striking instance of the effect of a constitution upon the life and events of a society. The constitution, created by the society, becomes a force which changes society.[12]

The Constitution becomes a revolutionary instrument, for Negroes, being political outcasts, have had to combat the government, and not merely the government of the day. Nowhere yet in the old Confederacy does a politically representative body debate and settle on policy, except in two circumstances: to shore up the legal defenses of segregation; or to circumscribe as closely as possible the scope of a judicial decree when defiance is considered inexpedient. Nowhere has a deliberative body accepted the premise that social change is necessary or inevitable, and that action to guide that change is its responsibility.

None has done so, because southern political theory has been incapacitating. Although formal democracy has been in short supply in the South, the tone and practice of southern politics has been democratic almost to an extreme—among the whites. Probably no where else in the country have there been closer personal relationships between voters and representatives, at all levels of government. But a democracy which is short on formal controls and efficient methods of obtaining popular consensus, and which puts a high value on informal means of effecting accountability, is going to be a conservative society. And when not all the inhabitants are constituents, the conservatism will be, in fact, defensiveness. Thus both the democratic and the conservative spirits of the South combined to defend the folk, its monopoly of power and its cultural integrity. There is nothing to deliberate about, and to do so is betrayal. There is no relief from this paralysis except through an enlarged Negro vote, and a few municipalities of the South are already tasting this emancipation.

We may well ask again whether, when a conflict runs deep, democratic politics and its institutions can solve it. If the southern conflict is being resolved, it is because it was possible to appeal it to a constitution, whose first principle is that it itself is enforceable law. There is still some life left in the old maxim that democracy requires agreement on fundamentals, although it may more accurately be this: that democratic politics cannot be counted on to bridge deep chasms of opinions and values unless undergirded by a fundamental authority (e.g., a self-enforcing constitution) which is independent of parties and legislatures.

Impersonal causes—the boll weevil, farm technology and chemicals, faster-paced industrialization, communications media, and still others—re-arranged the roots of southern life after World War I. But human action did not, until the last decade.

Now Southerners are not only being moved by their environment, but are revising themselves and their manners of living with and getting along with each other. Events and change are pell-mell, and unpredictable. Whatever we say, we must say most tentatively. I note, therefore, that the case has often, even usually, been that white Southerners can and do change their racial mores when inescapably confronted by a community-wracking situation to which they must respond in one way or another. But I note further that this has not been invariably so; witness, e.g., Albany (Ga.). Those places, however, which have refused to yield to the Negro demands, modest as they often have been in the South, have been able to do so only through techniques of suppression which tear at precepts of the Constitution. They have maltreated the right of assembly, denigrated the supremacy of federal law, whored the police powers of the states.

The Negro demands have been within the Constitution. The Negro methods have been within the liberties and privileges of the Constitution; only occasionally have they violated the rules of the game. Southern communities have been tested, therefore, not only in their customs and morality, but in their understanding of and affection for the Constitution. Those many which have accommodated, and have stepped into the currents of change, have shown to us that the feelings men have do not necessarily determine their actions or reactions; that when confronted with practical choices, men discover themselves more accurately than they had before. I have to leave to others the scientific analysis,[13] but I believe we can see the mind of the white South changing through the action of the black South and the accommodating reaction of the white South, and that a new South is shaping itself through history-making, and not through history-consciousness.

Success breeds hard problems, and it seems to me that the Negro movement is courting two very serious ones. There is disquieting evidence that a great many Negroes, naturally imbued with the excitement and the power of having led America's first sustained experiment in government by the street, are oblivious to the fact that their guiding rule and their indispensable ally has been the Constitution. Secondly, the availability of the political process has been so long withheld from them that they may not learn soon to value it.

I see little or no prospect for rational answers to America's or the South's racial woes unless the channels of politics are opened up for their resolution, by Congress and by the states. This means a steady transference of issues from court to legislature. The Constitution has done its work, and the way is cleared to reach decisions through consensus. For the long run, *Baker v. Carr* may be the avenue through which Negroes, under the leadership and representation of new, political types, may bring racial issues finally into political settlement. In the nature of things, the South's practical alternative to government by the street may include the price of a half dozen or more Adam Clayton Powells, but that is democracy's age-old exaction.

In the meantime, we can note that any government has but three possible postures toward the question of racial equality: in favor, opposed, or neutral. The political theory of the South has for more than three centuries been grounded on the principle of white supremacy. It has been the cardinal doctrine. If, then, southern state governments were to follow the lead already given by some municipalities, and move from opposition to neutrality, this would be a truly historic change.

In fact, the border states have already moved beyond neutrality,[14] and have begun incorporating into their public policy commitments favoring equality. And of even greater historic moment, some of the old Confederacy states have begun the withdrawal of state power from the defense of segregation and inequality.

This seems to me the *sine qua non* for the preservation of the South, as a community of persons acknowledging a common heritage. There must be an end to governmental hostility toward Negro advance, and acceptance of a political theory which sees government as neutral toward the competing aspirations of all economic and social elements. Such theory has been a commonplace in American national politics since at least Theodore Roosevelt. It will have to be established in the South and will have to be founded on the conditional truth that neutrality of the governmental power has to exist if there is to be order. Hobbes may not have said the last word in political philosophy, but he did say the first: power should be independent of the competition of private interests, and, because of its recognition of the equal potential threat of every person to public order, must acknowledge the equality of rights.

V

Let us say only that as long as a large number of people sense an identity among themselves, the South as a specific, self-conscious culture will endure. As was said at the start of this essay, who is there who is not tired of struggles for more definitive answers?[15] Perhaps I could venture that a Southerner is a person who feels, as against all other people, that he is the more moral, using that word in its broadest meaning of being spiritually fit for life as it is. But this would say no more than that the Southerner shares a widespread conceit. Perhaps it would mean more if I said that the Southerner is someone who can recognize that he has lost every argument about good and evil he has ever had—and he's had a lot—yet he *still* feels himself somehow more moral, again in the broadest meaning.

But it is safer to come back to the simple test of identification. The deepest wisdom in human relations is to accept a man as whatever he names himself. Ten years from now, or 20, will people living between the Potomac and the Rio Grande still identify themselves with each other, still feel worthwhileness in calling themselves Southerners?

I don't know. But I think we all do know some things that bear on the answer.

We know, most importantly, that politics is the way a people conducts its affairs, and that politics not only serves a group of people pragmatically but gives it unity, helps make of it a community. When the political processes cannot handle the affairs of the people, and when to settle grievances men have to act outside those processes, the polity is always hurt, sometimes to the point of death. Both Negroes and intense segregationists, including segregationist officials, have felt that they must take their causes outside the normal processes of politics.

The South is a little place. It cannot act greatly, and its survival means hardly anything to the world. Except that, as I have tried to argue, the only way it can, in fact, survive is to do something that *would* matter to the world, and that is to become a rarity, a bi-racial community at peace with itself. It can do so, I think, only by integrating Negroes into its political processes.

Southern politics is just now, as usual, full of curious things. Mississippi is experimenting with a Soviet style government, with the Citizens Council paralleling the state machine in emulation of a successful Communist Party. Southern governors have become the *de facto* executive directors of the state chambers of commerce, and spend their time competing with each other as supplicants for new plants. We have talked of state socialism and state capitalism, but what do we call governments whose chief affair it is to entice and propitiate business? And all over the South, battle lines draw close to each other, portentous of an epic contest which may never occur in any explicit, decisive engagement, but which will, one way or another, reach to the innermost desires of the South.

For southern conservatism is blending now with that of the nation at large in spirited defense against the dissolution of the old unities of American life. Southern liberalism has, and this is its good luck, no choice but to accept the Negro's cause as its own. The pains of the warfare between those who are rebelling against 300 years of history and those who want to move more rapidly into the future, will probably be most acutely felt in the South; it is the South's ancient calling to deflect pain and guilt from the rest of the nation.

Negroes have hymned the American dream, but only its battlecries. There are other parts of it and, if we read our history honestly, the Birchites and lesser breeds within the law are responsive to them. A "nice" home; people like ourselves; Jesus, and "our" church; the righteousness of property. America is on its way, not to a confrontation with its dream, but to a study of it, a mining of its content. The cutting edge of one drill is the radical right, and the other is the Negroes. It is in the South that each will probably cut most deeply. We are likely to learn a lot about ourselves, these next few years, as the drills cut away.

4

An Excerpt from My Foreword to *Climbing Jacob's Ladder: The Arrival of Negroes in Southern Politics*

1967

My Foreword is not reprinted in its entirety. Much of it seems no longer pertinent, and sometimes mistaken. Nevertheless, this present book being its own kind of history, essential aspects of the civil rights days would be missing without these views. The months after the Voting Rights Act changed the movement in important ways. (I dated here the Movement's demise in 1966, which seems rather arbitrary. In some lectures I gave in 2000, I ventured that the Movement withered away during the first Nixon administration.)

Some would say—with much reason—that the civil right movement came to its end between the summer of 1965 and the spring of 1966. . . . [A] variety of suddenly congregating influences . . . combined to weaken the movement from within while reducing the nation's tolerance of and interest in it and its mission.

In rough chronological order there was first the passage in July of the Voting Rights Act of 1965 which, following on the Civil Rights Act of 1964, represented the fulfillment of the prime articulated demands (*not* the goals) of the movement, and also transferred initiative for further advance against the classical problems of voter, educational, employment, and service discrimination from the movement itself to the federal government. Moreover, by summer 1965, the federal anti-poverty program was beginning to unfold and to be felt. Many from the leadership cadre of the movement lessened their concentration on grand goals and threw themselves into struggle over the nature and control of local community action programs. Something else entered here too: jobs. The anti-poverty program of the 1960's has not been a mass producer of jobs, but it has bred a sizable lot of positions for administrators, organizers, and research and information people. For the first time, there was patronage available and seeking for precisely the kinds of persons who had staffed the civil rights organizations.

On the heels of the Voting Rights Act came Watts. The riot there—and the others that sprang up elsewhere—did undoubtedly shatter the nerve and increase the resistance of many whites. Some liberals were scared off. But the movement of 1960–65 had overcome other serious crises of popular confidence; riots in Northern cities had been also bad in 1964; and for as long as one can remember the culpable inadequacy of "liberals" has been a favorite conversation piece of the movement. A greater harm of Watts was that the civil rights leadership was unprepared for it and stayed confused by it. The civil rights laws had transferred much of the responsibility for further tangible progress to the White House; now in their blurred response to Watts, the movement's leadership forfeited large portions of the tremendous moral leadership it then had. It could not either accept or effectively repudiate "Burn, baby, burn," and could never find a way to escape that either/or. And so the civil rights movement lapsed from its magnificent expressiveness into loud unintelligibility.

The White House Conferences in November 1965 and May 1966 seem, in retrospect, not only failures but disasters, because they forced people who desperately and above all, at that period, needed a private time to find new thoughts, to nag at each other in a lurid spotlight, and to drag down a lovely, cleanly phrased movement into a whirlpool of sullen meaningless talk, from which rescue has hardly yet begun. This was the backdrop of the fatuous "black power" controversy. In all our history, no Americans ever acted with more dignity and—yes—style than those who led the way from Selma to Montgomery. Less than a year later, that movement which they had led and for which they had spoken was shattered, and large elements of it were driving pell-mell toward a new era, an era of the chant rather than the song, of the incantation rather than the thought, of the buffoon instead of the hero, and of an explicit rejection of the movement's holy things—love, integration, and respect for the person.

... Yet I am not sure that the movement could not have withstood all else had it not been for the hectic increase during this same period of the Vietnam war. No wistful or demagogic—as the case might be—contentions that we could as a nation pay the costs of both a large-scale war in a distant land and a systematic drive against discrimination and poverty could conceal the truth that we would not do it; nor would there be any relevance to self-serving claims that we *would* have, had only others not acted badly and unwisely. It seems clear now that when the President's celebrated "peace offensive" collapsed in the early weeks of 1966, the civil rights movement was impliedly dissolved, its revolution effectively terminated. The churning moral and political dilemmas of that war chewed up its clear-sightedness and relentless advance. ...

If we try to make clear what we mean when we speak of the "civil rights movement," I think we must say that it was defined by Southern problems and given character by the qualities of Negro Southerners. The movement did, of course, spread beyond the South, but always the cohesion was the South. The Northerners who came down to aid the Southern cause did not in the first years disturb the Southernness of its intellectual and spiritual thrust; indeed, part of the style of those workers from the North was a heartfelt wish to act and think as did their Negro hosts. The movement spoke and thought in an idiom that was about one half Biblical, and about one fourth each copy-book Americanism and social science—though the latter hardly got beyond the ritualistic and yet somehow sincerely felt incorporation of abstractions such as "the power structure" and "alienation." In time, the younger movement people popularized also existentialist themes, and then, as the movement began to breed cults and dark corners, some of them smothered it all in Dylanesque mockery.

But until then, the civil rights movement had been a very bright flame in American history, warming the hopes of a nation. The movement was never, however, illusionary. Watters and Cleghorn give heavy emphasis to the student wing of the movement, especially the Student Nonviolent Coordinating Committee. They are right to have done so because, though others may have registered far more voters or done or achieved other objective things, here within its student wing the movement distilled its essential character. SNCC did not by any means embrace all of the youth, and wherever students were, there was the same compound of idealism and hard thought, of fierceness and compassion, and, perhaps above all, of ingrained suspicion of broad programs and concern for individual cases. At the great Washington march of August 28, 1963, John Lewis, an Alabama farm boy who had become chairman of SNCC, spoke alongside the other leaders to the assembled throng and to the vast television audience. His prepared remarks had been read in advance by some of his colleagues and had upset their plans for the tone of the day; so they had pressed Lewis strongly to soften his speech, and he finally, with compassion and courtesy for them, complied. Here are some of the blunt, demanding, non-praising, old-SNCC style statements from his original manuscript.

> We march today for jobs and freedom, but we have nothing to be proud of.—
>
> In good conscience, we cannot support, wholeheartedly, the administration's civil rights bill, for it is too little, and too late. There's not one thing in the bill that will protect our people from police brutality.
>
> The voting section of this bill will not help thousands of black citizens who want to vote. It will not help the citizens of Mississippi, of Alabama, and Georgia, who are qualified to vote, but lack a sixth grade education. "One man, one vote," is the African cry. It is ours, too. . . . What is there in this bill to insure the equality of a maid who earns $5 a week in the home of a family whose income is $100,000 a year?
>
> We are now involved in a serious revolution. This nation is still a place of cheap political leaders who build their careers on immoral compromises and ally themselves with open forms of political, economic, and social exploitation. . . . The party of Kennedy is also the party of Eastland. The party of Javits is also the party of Goldwater. Where is *our* party?
>
> The revolution is at hand, and we must free ourselves of the chains of political and economic slavery. . . . We cannot depend on any political party, for both the Democrats and the Republicans have betrayed the basic principles of the Declaration of Independence.
>
> We all recognize the fact that if any radical social, political, and

economic changes are to take place in our society, the people, the masses, must bring them about. In the struggle we must seek more than mere civil rights; we must work for the community of love, peace, and true brotherhood. Our minds, souls, and hearts cannot rest until freedom and justice exist for *all the people.*

. . . Listen, Mr. Kennedy. Listen, Mr. Congressman, listen fellow citizens, the black masses are on the march for jobs and freedom . . .

We won't stop now. All of the forces of Eastland, Barnett, Wallace, and Thurmond won't stop this revolution. The time will come when we will not confine our marching to Washington. We will march through the South, through the heart of Dixie, the way Sherman did. We shall pursue our own "scorched earth" policy and burn Jim Crow to the ground—non-violently. We shall fragment the South into a thousand pieces and put them back together in the image of democracy. We will make the action of the past few months look pretty. And I say to you, WAKE UP AMERICA!!!

Climbing Jacob's Ladder explicates this Lewisan idealism-plus-hardness as it brightened and set to moving numberless persons of the South. I have quoted at some length, because the statement seems to me to recall clearly and well the tone and point of view of the civil rights movement at its peak, and that is to say, at the time chronicled by this book. Here was how the anger and the hope both were felt, even in days *before* the Birmingham bombing, the assassination of a believed-in President, the squalid brutality of St. Augustine, the Mississippi Summer of 1964, and all that happened in Selma and its aftermath.

The voter registration campaign was not the whole of the civil rights movement, but it expressed it all. The movement we knew is over but it had an intrinsic worth, independent of how it may have changed its future or shaped our present. But though the movement never did "fragment the South" and put it "back together in the image of democracy," it did make of the South and the nation a greatly different land. In the doing of that, the voter registration campaign had the biggest part.

The civil rights movement, as we knew it in the early sixties, is ended. The grand assemblage held together by a determination to erase the Southern blight is no more. Whether it can reassemble for other crusades is a question for the future. To say that the civil rights movement is over is not to say, however, that the Second Reconstruction of the South is ended. On that, I am more the optimist than is C. Vann Woodward in his celebrated article, "What Happened to the Civil Rights Movement?" (*Harper's Magazine*, January 1967). I believe that at the worst the evidence is still coming in, and that such evidence as we now have shows that, despite everything epitomized by the Wallaces of Alabama, the South is now and will continue to be a different and better place. What made the crucial difference, what made it possible to cross the border into a social order where a just multiracial society is now a true possibility was the civil rights movement. That that movement is now in disarray does not change the fact that it was a magnificent success. . . .

5

Remarks to the National Civil Liberties Clearing House

1968

The War Against Vietnam dominated the second half of the 1960s, to the disfavor of the cause of civil rights and of the "war against poverty." I was a traditional patriot when it began, inclined to trust that there must be some way of "understanding" its purpose. I remember being in the fall of 1965 at the University of Michigan, where I was speaking, and wandering one night into a hall where Dwight MacDonald was lambasting the war and President Johnson. I was indignant: what right had he? Well, he was but a few months ahead of me. The war was and is a huge dark stain on American honor.

In March of 1968, I was trying to understand the liberal politics I had given my fealty to (and still, faut de mieux, do). The politics to which liberals had been wed since F.D.R. was going up in the flames of Vietnam, and naively or irrationally I here held out a belief that the students who had sustained both the civil rights movement and the movement against the war in Vietnam would endure as a political force. But, of course, at the terminus of all that had moved America in the 1960s stood the dead end of Richard Nixon, and, though "youth" would find many good things to do during the subsequent Age of Nixon, its days of leadership were done. The war against Vietnam would be the definitive event of those ensuing years. We live still in the war's wake—in the culture and values and political re-definitions it spawned.

I will return to the themes of this speech in the final essay, which is about the shattering year 1968.

It is not often that a private liberal is under a duty to acknowledge that politicians have been more right, indeed more constant, than he in serving the right. That is, I think, our duty now, because the small band of Senators who nourished the 1968 civil rights bill until they finally won for it an overwhelming majority in the Senate did so with very little stimulus or encouragement from the rest of us. These Senators were superb.

Humble as we must be in the face of their example, it is nevertheless worthwhile to ask if we private liberals have had any justification on our side. It seems to me there may have been a threefold cause for our lackadaisical performance and that its three sides may be the bounds of that crisis in race relations we are here discussing: we are tired, we are confused, and we are doubtful. We have only so much energy, and many are putting the best of themselves into the controversy over Vietnam or into the effort to save the anti-poverty programs. We have let the intellectual clarity of the pre-1966 civil rights movement erode into the frequent mindlessness and the paralyzingly dogmatic rivalries of the post-1965 period.

Fortunately, liberal Senators have not been so tired and confused as private liberals. On the other hand, the third cause of our inaction might possibly justify it as, of course, the first two do not. In addition to being tired and confused, we have become growingly doubtful of the value of certain traditional political solutions. American liberalism, at least during this century, has put its chief reliance for curing social problems on creating bureaucracies to regulate and, it is hoped, master them. It would not be far wrong to say that liberalism's motto has been, "A bureaucracy for every problem."

But to those who have seen so many bureaucracies created and yet so many problems endure, and who wonder therefore if the creation of another bureaucracy has practical relevance to the problem of housing discrimination, this is no longer the motto. Liberals who may be wondering about the lambasting we often get from our youth and from our more articulate poor might keep in mind what a deep identification we liberals have with the bureaucratic method. They, on the contrary, have a concern and even a fear about bureaucracies, or at least a strong wish (as exemplified in the controversies about parent involvement in the big city schools) for bureaucracies open to the easy passage of ideas and to entry by those persons who come from close to the heart of problems.

I think this brings us to the truth of the Black Power "cult." There is not much about this cult (and, of course, being a "cult" it is illiberal) which is helpful, and so we should give all the more weight to that which is. Insofar as Black Power invites and encourages vulgarity of thought and manners, or violence of thought and deed, or blesses racism, or luxuriates in irrationality, or breeds cheap leaders who march innocent people off into fantasy—insofar as it has done and continues to do all this, the cult of Black Power is another one of the enormous burdens that history has pushed down on Negro Americans.

But insofar as the Black Power people say—as they do say and are right in saying—that the political process does not work efficiently and that often it does not work even honestly when it addresses itself to the problems of the Negro poor, and insofar as the Black Power people say—as they do say and are right in saying—that the American government and people have false priorities, they add to the progressive forces of our time.

No government in the world is as internally complicated as our federal system, and to make it work, and work well, requires an extraordinarily able and interested citizenry. Consequently, I think no present trend is more supportive of constitutional government, as well as more hope-giving, than the urge toward experimentation in participatory democracy, for this offers a way out of our present tiredness, confusion, and suspicion.

The civil rights bill of 1968 will be tremendously beneficial for the added protection it gives to the lives and safety of civil rights workers and those exercising their civil rights, though the Department of Justice already has far more statutory authority and duty to protect these citizens than it has ever been willing to employ. The housing provisions of the bill mean a great deal, because they mark the first federal action whose main impact may be felt in the North, because they put the federal government forthrightly into the housing field, and because, in addition to these largely symbolic values, they will undoubtedly do also some good in curbing discrimination.

But this housing bill will not disperse the ghetto, and it will not undo the slum, and it will not, consequently, be seen as very important by the masses of Negroes and Puerto Ricans. I do not say this in any condescending or ungrateful spirit. I mean only that the ghettoized masses will probably not see or share in the value of this bill. It will not solve *their* housing problems. As the Kerner Commission noted, a federal anti-discrimination law is only the necessary beginning of an assault on the accursed living conditions of our enormous urban slums.[1]

It is terribly crucial that our government begin doing things that do not merely tease these masses. I am here, of course, only saying what has been many times said, and what all of you probably believe. Let me indulge in just a few more clichés. Comprehensive, curative, effective things have got to be done with these urban masses because: (a) their own need as human beings is so intense and so justified, and (b) they are in their present condition a threat to the peace of all of us.

These are, to repeat, clichés; they happen also to be inescapable truths, but I shall not be exploring them further today. Instead, speaking here in this gathering of liberals, I want to say that we cannot be at all sure that these urban masses will be a progressive political force. The Negroes of the vast Harlem, Watts, Chicago, and other northern slums are today acting in a variety of ways that frequently cancel out each other's impact and often intensify white opposition without any approximately equivalent yield of benefits. They may over the next few years continue this way, in which case we shall have a politics of disorder and repression—or they may allow themselves to be captured by political machines held in other and mostly white hands. In neither of these cases will they be anything but an illiberal, even destructive, force.

Our hope has to be that these northern and western urban masses will take a third course, that they will produce a kind of political leadership that will represent the interests of their constituents with dignity and with unrelenting purpose. This kind of Negro political leadership is emerging in the South, and if it does not come more rapidly forth in the North and the West we are as a nation in real trouble.

Politics—American politics—is always a matter of alliances. What alliances will most likely represent the progressive forces of the next generation or so? The rest of my talk will, in one way or another, be underlining certain beliefs about that. First, since New Deal days American liberalism has been expressed by an alliance of labor, Negroes, and a hard to define but huge population of well-educated individualists. If the Vietnam policies of the administration do not change, this historic alliance will not last out 1968. Second, the historic alliance is, in any event, subject to basic probes from two sides: one comes from the no longer inert and obedient minority poor, who are getting too little—some would say, nothing—from the alliance; the other comes from students, who are subjecting the institutions of the republic to passionate as well as intelligent scrutiny. My third belief is that the constant itch of liberals to "reach" and "involve" business must surely be expressive of some deep cultural myth about tribal gods and how to propitiate them. Although one would think that businessmen are grown up enough to find their own way of doing their duty, liberals invest hugely of their scarce energy in seeking to guide and direct them in the ways of virtue. One who remembers Plans for Progress in 1961, and the White House conferences of 1963, and the national committee brought together by the Community Relations Service in 1964 is entitled to some skepticism now about the Urban Coalition; one begins to wonder if business is like the old-time sinner, needing to be saved and consecrated anew at every revival.

My fourth belief is that the progressive forces of our time are, if they are anything, the minority poor and the left-wing or liberal students. Does it make sense to speak of students as a political interest group? Well, I think it probably does. I am using the word as a shorthand designation for educated youth, politically oriented from dissenting Democrats leftward. They have these last few years acted as a self-generating, self-propelling force to reform American society, and that is more than can be said for labor or business or some other interest groups. Since 1960, the other great self-generating, self-propelling forces have been Negro Southerners and the nationwide civil rights movement. The movement is, as I suggested earlier, in such a confused and tired state as to be no longer very forceful. So I am inclined to think that whatever vigor and sense of purpose American society will have in the next decade or so will depend on the quality of leadership that comes to us from these disadvantaged minorities.

I believe, furthermore, that this has deep implications for American liberals, for it comes at a time when we face a probable division.

We are assembled here as representatives of American liberalism in our belief that whatever disagreements there may be among us, they are less than the agreements which unite us. There is a very good chance that Vietnam and the foreign policy which produces it are about to break apart our unity, that, in other words, the conflict among us during this election year will not pass but will permanently break the coalition of labor, minority groups, and individualists who have since New Deal days been the standard bearers of liberalism.

I want to return to that in a few minutes. Before I do, I would like to look a little longer at traditional liberalism. Beginning with Theodore Roosevelt, we have had two-thirds of a century in which one wave of domestic reform has followed another, and where are we now? We are at a time when at least one of five of us is miserably poor, when racial discrimination is rampant, when our streets are unsafe, when we arm our police as if the Russians were coming, when our big-city schools are incapable of teaching and our welfare departments are incapable of stopping the increase of needy cases, and when even hunger stalks the land. Has liberalism failed? Or does liberalism give with the hand of domestic reform and take away with the hand of foreign war?

We must face ourselves and concede that it is precisely those administrations that have led in domestic reforms that have also led us into wars. Is there a schizophrenia of liberalism? Are we—we here today as the representatives of American liberalism—the true and essential warmongers of the land? Can it be that only liberals could feel sure enough of the rightness of their purposes to make the kind of war we have now in Vietnam? What do we make of the fact that so very many of the old New Dealers still around are the staunchest hawks of the Democratic party? That this war apparently has the approval of most of organized labor?

If these questions are in bad taste, then so too was the Kerner Commission's charge that white racism envelops this land. There come times when we have to look at ourselves with honest vision. This is such a time. We are killing people, our own and those of a faraway nation. That is the most important fact of our times. President Johnson, who says that we are killing people for a just cause, is a better man than those other liberals who apologize for it all but say other things are more important just now.

We must accept the fact that this war divides us, as it fractures all our public life. If this and any other meeting where liberals gather together is not relevant to the war in Vietnam, it is simply not relevant. So far, it is principally those of us who are against that war who say that it dominates every public issue, while those not yet active against it would prefer to focus on other issues. But later, my friends, if this war goes much longer, it will be, I fear, its defenders who will say, as its critics say today, "The war comes first"—but with quite a different meaning.

The old union song called out, "Which side are you on, boys?" We may be apart a good while. For Vietnam is the expression of a foreign policy that can, and will if it is not curbed, produce more Vietnams. The issue is whether the great powers, of which we are one and probably the greatest, will attune their power to the world or try to force the world to fit their power. Before Vietnam, liberals could and did squabble and scrap, but only Vice President Humphrey believes that the present division is of that same gentle kind.

I read Irving Kristol's recent piece in the [February 11, 1968,] *New York Times Magazine:* "Memoirs of a Cold Warrior." He was an important, I a most unimportant, anti-Communist liberal of the 1950s; but like him, I have no regrets and some small pride in what we stood for and what we did. Yet when he talked in that article of the attacks he and other anti-Communist liberals endured from what he calls the anti-anti-Communist liberals, I could not share the memory. His experience was in New York literary and intellectual circles. Out in the ranks, we only read about that. I remember the 1950s as a time of marvelous unanimity among liberals. We agreed with each other about everything, about Joe McCarthy, and Nixon, and Dixon-Yates, and Oppenheimer, and Dulles, and civil rights (which meant we all favored moving ahead on the next target selected by the NAACP lawyers), and all the rest. Conversation was lovely, friendships abounded. Eisenhower made us "one from many."

Now (though in my worst dreams I see some flickering evidence that President Johnson has in his own way brought about and embodies the longed-for union of labor and Negroes) we are divided. The divisions have to do essentially with the uses of national power and the cause of the poor, the truly poor, the poor that the New Deal and all that has followed never did reach.

In those far-off Eisenhower years, Adlai Stevenson gave meaning to our public life. What we saw and recognized in him was what we believed to be America. He may have been denied the power he was ready to accept, but few men have meant so much to so many as for six to eight years he meant to us. As he was our leader, Camus and Orwell were our philosophers and prophets, and E.B. White was our weekly comforter. Did ever anyone have better mentors?

In one way or another we moved away from each of them as we went into the Kennedy years and the great days of the civil rights movement, though I think they helped many of us find our way through those times. Now they seem again real and close, as we see that nothing is so wanted of us as clear heads and clear decisions about the use of power. Our students may be Dr. Spock's children. Those of us who learned to be adult from Stevenson, Orwell, Camus, and E.B. White have, I like to think, an equal disposition toward reason and self-awareness, an equal fear of confusing presumption with principle, an equal hope that we may someday learn to be gentle of spirit and act.

The Black Power people and the more traditional civil rights organizations have much the same goal; it is, in the vernacular, "getting ahead," or, in the newer vernacular, "making it." The traditional organizations want Negroes to "get ahead" as individuals and the Black Power people seem to want them to do it as a group. A white man can and should respond to the former. I am at a loss to see how we can, on their own terms, respond to the Black Power people except to say, "Okay, good luck, go ahead and do it." To both, however, to traditionalists and to Black Power cultists, the white person can, in the final analysis, respond only as a white person.

In our time there has been a third approach, one that still is alive among a remnant of old SNCC and CORE and SCLC workers and friends, white and Negro, and among some Negro and white liberals who were moved and changed by it. It believes that we can and ought to transform society, that, although we cannot fully sense how that can be done or to what ends, it can be done by black and white together, that in that union, in that reconciliation, America could at last discover itself and the texture of its ancient dream. To this one could, whether Negro or white, respond, simply and completely, as a man or as a woman.

What those old SNCC and SCLC and CORE people did was marvelous. They taught us not to care—really not to care—about color. Nothing good has ever, will ever, or can ever come from color identity. I shall call anybody anything he wants to be called. If my Negro friends want me to call them Blacks, they have only to ask and I'll unfalteringly do it. I wish, however, we had not had to go through this one. I wish Negro Americans had said to us instead: "Color is out. You may not call us Blacks or Browns or Coloreds and we don't want to call you Whites either. We would rather call you something which, like the word 'Negro,' has some meaning in your history, is something from your culture that you can identify with, like, maybe, Crackers, or Honkies." "Let us," I wish Negro Americans had said, "no longer sing 'black and white together, we shall overcome.' Let us instead sing, out of our self-awareness, our humbling self-knowledge of what we have been and how we have wronged ourselves and each other, out of our knowledge that we are people with history and culture that defines us and limits us and yet which we must overcome and transform, let us sing, 'Negroes and Honkies together, we shall overcome.'"

This calls up old dreams from an old time. There is a place in the New Testament where God speaks to his church and says "Fortitude you have; you have borne up in my cause and never flagged. But I have this against you: you have lost your early love" (Revelation 2:3-4 [New English]). So it is perhaps with us. The "early love" that gave us self-awareness during the great days of the civil rights movement, where is it now? If it is gone or wavering, let us know that it did not fail, but rather that we failed it. John Morris, in a wonderful speech he gave a short time ago, spoke of the American Dream and said that we had, in all truth, dreamed it *in all our history* for only a few years in the early 1960s. I suppose we pull back always from our dreams. But the dream itself neither dies nor fades, even though its popularity may, and some who have envisioned it can never lose it from their sight.

If the historic alliance of labor, Negroes, and educated individualists can function today as a way of reordering national priorities and the values that lie at the root of our discontent, then it will be truly worth one's loyalty. If the historic alliance does do this it will be because it will have succeeded in opening itself to the entry of the truly poor and has in realistic ways made their cause its own.

The historic alliance has become an affluent, a privileged, a highly placed class. It cannot preserve liberalism by preserving itself alone. It can preserve a liberal—i.e., a free—political order only by being willing to lead in those structural changes of this society that will make possible the rescue of the minority poor.

In my belief, the old alliance will not be able to do this unless foreign policy ceases to dominate us. If we go on as we are now headed, that alliance will be shattered beyond repair.

In that event, that all too likely event, liberals will have to set about building new alliances. And we do well to remember that the real strength of liberalism is not embodied in any institutions or institutional groupings. It is, in our time, vested in a vast gathering of individuals. To put it crassly, this is where the votes are, not in union headquarters and not in denominational bureaucracies. Liberals may or may not be trade unionists or share interests with them; they may or may not be churchgoers and church adherents; [they] may or may not feel an identity with business; [they] may or may not feel a concern for the prosperity of the universities. I think no mistake would be worse than the one that would lead us to identify the liberal cause with that of any institution or groups of [institutions].

The liberal cause is the cause of the disadvantaged, the poor, the shirtless ones. It is also the cause of peace. It is also the cause of free thought and free speech. That is the beginning and the end of it. Let those who see it so coalesce with us.

6

Remarks to the Mississippi Council on Human Relations

1975

Why include old speeches in this collection? One reason is that they were contemporary, packed with the spirit and concerns of their times. This book is in no sense a proper history or a memoir. I do, however, want it to be evocative of the days of the civil rights movement and its denouement and aftermath. I believe the few speeches included here may in a measure help achieve that. The "great contest going on" within America, told of in the opening paragraph of this speech, is still an ongoing fact, for better or worse.

This old 1970s talk, besides expressing my admiration of some people who get too little recognition, namely, African-American and white liberals who had banded together in "human relations councils," also expressed my despisal of the breed of southern politicians—and it is not yet extinct—who were the upholders of white supremacy. The address spoke also to my then, and continuing, skepticism that reform could reliably depend on litigation.

That skepticism extended then as it does now to the course followed by the federal courts for the integration of minorities—African and Hispanic Americans—into the public schools, putting the burden on the children themselves. There must have been, must be, better ways.

I am glad to be here, with old friends and new, and to freeload this way on what is one of the sustaining forces of American democracy in the 1970s, by which I mean the stubborn struggle of you free people of Mississippi to make a good state and a good place to live. It has often seemed to me the last few years that America has a great contest going on within itself, and how it may turn out I don't know. I do know that never in our lifetime have there been so many and such strong powers, political, economic, and technological, driving us toward a world unfit for human enjoyment, if not for life itself. But never in our lifetime has there also been seen such determined and intelligent striving for freedom and equality, for peace, and for the care of our natural environment. In that vision of clashing forces, the work you are doing to transform Mississippi, to make of it a place of civility and freedom, has a right to special value and historic meaning.

I take personal pleasure too in following my longtime friends, Robert Coles and Will Campbell,[1] who spoke to your annual meetings the past two years. I hope that I have a number of things in common with Bob and Will, and among them is that, one way or the other, each of us has been deeply etched by our experience in and of Mississippi. I spoke once before at your annual meeting—it was in 1964, at the old King Edward Hotel, and it was the first time we had all, black and white, been able to gather in downtown Jackson. It was one of those lovely, wonderful events that in the 1960s used now and then to lift us from the tensions of those times and seemed to show to us that we were winning.

Such warming experiences don't happen often anymore. We are having to make do without drama, and the great thing about you in Mississippi has been that, even though here the drama was most intense and the letdown might have been the sharpest, you have, on the contrary, steadily kept at your work. At the Southern Regional Council, before 1961, we worried about Alabama and Arkansas and Georgia and South Carolina and all the rest of the South—but not Mississippi. Too hard! And then Robert Moses and a few others from SNCC, in the wake of the Freedom Rides and encouraged by the longtime earlier work of Aaron Henry, Medgar Evers, and the NAACP, moved into McComb and then later, still putting their lives at risk, up to the Delta. Not only has Mississippi never been the same since, not only have the South and the country not been the same, but perhaps even more important, not since then have we known fear as we knew it before

1961, and not since then have we acceptably excused ourselves from doing what has to be done because the odds seem too high. When SNCC went into Mississippi, they set the example that persuaded a few others in 1965 and 1966 that they ought to, and therefore could, stop an insane war against the Vietnamese people. The peace movement, and after it the other liberating movements of today's America, grew from the seeds sown in the heat of a Mississippi spring and summer. A lot of us, and maybe the nation too, came of age in Mississippi, in the sense that we learned to face what we had to do, learned not to excuse ourselves from attempting to do it, and began to put out of our heads many fairy tales and cruel myths about southern and American history.

Some of you—all of you, I hope—caught my allusion just then to Anne Moody's book *Coming of Age in Mississippi*, one of a handful of truly valued writings about the South. Some years ago, another Mississippian, William Alexander Percy, wrote his book about growing up in Mississippi, a sweet and appealing story. But *Lanterns on the Levee* was a book whose teaching was that men must live by myths. Anne Moody knew that we had to grow up, and she and those other students in the early 1960s taught us how.

I have something else in common with Will Campbell and Bob Coles. We are all three white. Up in New York, such people as we are now called "others." Statistically, New York divides its population into blacks, Spanish speaking, Orientals—and "others." Thus, for example, in the Bronx, where about one and one-half million people live, two-thirds as many as in all Mississippi, there are about 360,000 blacks, 410,000 Spanish speaking—mainly Puerto Ricans—and about 600,000 "others." Despite that plurality, it may interest you to know that next fall's projections are that in seven of the Bronx's thirteen public high schools, "others" will be 10 percent or less of enrollment. In fact, in only three schools is there expected to be a white majority, one of those being the prestigious Bronx High School of Science. The situation is getting close to that of Atlanta and Memphis, whose schools now are mainly black.

Well, this business of terminology is interesting, when it isn't confusing. Some of us have drifted from being colored, to Negro, to black; some of us have gone from white to "others." "I'm white" gets replaced by "I'm another," which perhaps, to some, means the same.

My references to the Bronx schools are, of course, to a situation that prevails twenty years after the Supreme Court ordered the desegregation of schools "with all deliberate speed." We learned, to our bitter shame, what that could mean at the hands of southern politicians, a race of men to whom, by and large, we owe no respect. More recently, we have seen that northern school systems can be even more sly and as unfeelingly clever in resisting desegregation. And of all the northern stories, that of Boston is the most marvelous in its long, drawn-out, step-by-step obstruction that any southern "massive resister" might admiringly envy.

I don't make these remarks about New York and Boston in order to indulge in the fruitless game of massaging southern pride by pointing, as is all too easy to do, to northern wrongs and faults. I've said them in order to say that there is harshness everywhere and that a society which cared for children would have done better.

The greatest of all hardships that this society imposes on its children is that it has no jobs for so many of their parents and badly inadequate jobs for so many more. Unemployment now is upwards of eight million and rising; in New York City, even by the official counts, it has now reached 11.5 percent of the working force. The National Urban League convincingly estimates that 25 percent of black workers are lacking full-time jobs and that the rate for black teenagers is 40 percent. There is only so much that even the best services for children could do for children gripped in that kind of dismal family economics.

No recital of other states' or the nation's villainy toward children can hide Mississippi's own. Here, for black children there is the highest infant mortality rate in the country, 39.7 per 1,000 (which is, incidentally, twice as high as Mississippi's white rate). The state has dragged its feet vilely on the Women, Infants, and Children (WIC) food program, with only seven projects approved after two and a half years. Treatment of mentally retarded children is so shot through with inequities that the Community Legal Services, supported by the Children's Defense Fund, has brought suit against Whitfield Mental Hospital and the Oakley Training School; and now last week's lawsuit brought by the Children's Defense Fund has shown how indifferent the state and its school districts are to the rights and needs of handicapped children, particularly those who are black. Mississippi's aid to dependent children is the lowest in the country. The state refuses to put any money at all into Title IVA social services programs. Nearly 8 percent of your children are not enrolled in school. Yours is the only state in the country without a compulsory school attendance law. Mississippi's outstanding Head Start programs have had fierce opposition, relieved now and then by indifference, from your state government, and never the slightest support from it in their just plea for increased funds; we are, in Washington, apparently about to adopt the rule—for the first and only time, so far as I know, in federal appropriations—that an inflationary factor is to be built into the Pentagon's appropriation—none, it hardly needs mentioning, is allowed for Head Start or other services for children. Whatever cooperation your state government has given to day care centers has been wrested from it after struggle by the Mississippi Federation for Early Childhood Education. Your state Textbook Commission, in order to bar the children of this state from reality, has kept from their classrooms Jim Loewen and Charles Sallis's fine text on Mississippi history.

But we must not lose sight of the other side of all this. The State of Mississippi would not have so many opportunities to obstruct better care for the state's children if so many of you were not so effectively pressing their cause. And you will know, and I'm sure are working on, the answer to such questions as the extent of coverage by the Early and Periodic Screening Diagnosis and Treatment Program; the conditions of children in foster and institutional care, and who is accountable and how for them; and whether your juvenile courts, where they exist, do and are enabled to help children brought before them.

So I think the best thing Mississippi does for its children is what you have led the state to do or have done yourselves. And even more than your tangible achievements has been the example of caring, of courage, of just and honorable values which you have shown to the children. For I have always believed that children learn more from what adults are than from what they do for them.

On the same day last week (April 24), the *New York Times* carried [two] items that say a lot about what our contemporary society honors, and thereby tries to teach young people to emulate. At the annual stockholders' meeting of General Electric, the chairman defended his salary of $501,200—up from $312,528 in 1973—by saying that some rock musicians make more. And Revlon hired a new president at a salary of $325,000 *plus* a bonus of $1.5 million, *plus* options to buy 70,000 shares at $27 a share below market price; that's even better than Catfish Hunter did.

So I think also that the worst of what the other side of Mississippi society does for children is not its neglect of them, but the values and attitudes it teaches them. When a society elects and re-elects a James Eastland and a John Stennis, it is very clearly telling the children of the state what kind of person it wants them to become. And, ladies and gentlemen, they are being given an awful message! Your Senators have fought, at every governmental level and with every means, Head Start, aid to dependent children, school feeding programs, and every other social service and benefit for children. I cannot believe there is or has been a child anywhere in the United States who owes a word of thanks to the public acts of these men. But more than that, they have—and I sadly cannot believe that the example has been missed by young people growing up in this state—set their power *against* every measure proposed for civil rights and civil liberties and *for* the curtailment of the government's secret police; and they have worked incessantly for ever stronger destructive forces. A reported $590,000,000 is being spent in fiscal year 1975 by the Pentagon for *recruitment*. That is three times the cost of the Washington, D.C. schools. Senators Eastland and Stennis stand for a government without mercy and without care and with an infinite capacity to police our own citizens and to kill those of foreign lands. While they stay in office, they are this state's profoundest, its most telling, teaching to its children.

They, of course, are not alone. What lessons many children and youth of this state—and the South—must have been taught as they have seen parents, church bodies, community leaders, and teachers organize, build, and operate the segregationist private academies! There are said to be one hundred and fifty of them in Mississippi, with a number of the most thriving here in Hinds County.

What is the status of school desegregation in Mississippi, as you see it and not necessarily as the statistics show it? For the South as a whole, it seems to me, from the secondhand things I read, that the status could be summed up by three statements:

- the public schools are, from the standpoint of equal opportunity, better than they have been;
- but they don't seem to be getting any better;
- and the chances of their sliding back are a bit better than the chances of further advance.

I believe it is time that we ask ourselves what further we want from the legal process of school desegregation, or of integration—though I have never known what that word means, and it seems to be only vaguely understood by anyone. Surely we should begin that inquiry by agreeing upon the purposes of public schools. To my mind, they are chiefly three: To enable children and young people to learn, to think more clearly and creatively, and to develop their bodies and personalities healthily. That is the primary, and emphatically the most important purpose of schools. To it we can add two others. One of those is that the schools are one of the prime institutions that knit people together into communities. A basic fault of all private schools, whether Exeter or a Citizens Council school in Jackson, is that they make no contribution at all to the building of the practice and the spirit of community. That New York City is today lurching from one crisis of decaying civic life to another is due in no small part to the fact that in Manhattan and widely throughout the rest of the city, the middle class and up—black as well as white—have largely quit the public school system. A third purpose that public schools serve is providing a place and an opportunity for teachers and others to work, and with dedication to seek better ways of helping children to learn and grow.

Before *Brown v. Topeka*, when schools were rigidly segregated, none of these three purposes was achievable in the South. Segregated schools were not places where children could learn and develop well. They divided the society rather than helping to knit it together. They put teachers into situations where professional growth was stunted by the prevention of communication and experience across racial lines.

Brown v. Topeka declared the Constitution's meaning, that children could not by law be assigned to school on the basis of race. It thereby opened the way for all of the three purposes of schools I have suggested to be achieved, even though the road to them would be a long one. The opposition of southern politicians and the ill will typically shown by southern business chieftains and the lack of principle and love within southern white churches long frustrated, and still does impede, the hopes that *Brown v. Topeka* made possible. Without the support of political and civic leadership, the federal courts had to shoulder virtually the entire burden, prior to 1965 and once again since about 1970, of bringing about the desegregation of southern schools. In that process, they—joined by federal courts of the North—have extended *Brown v. Topeka* to hold, in effect, that when laws or other official acts of the past resulted in children being placed in schools according to race, children must now, under some circumstances, be *assigned by race* in order to undo past discrimination.

I happen to think that this was the wrong turn for the law to take and one that has led it into dreadfully difficult problems of enforcement. I think a better direction, and one it seems to me clearly consistent with *Brown*, would have been to have affirmed the individual right of a minority child not only against assignment by race but against assignment to a school whose performance is not up to the state's own averages. I think *Brown* should also have been applied, as it clearly could have been, to forbid any governmental cooperation at all with any private school not truly open to all races.

The courts went, however, in that other direction, of requiring the re-shaping of school systems in pursuit of the greatest degree possible of racial integration, even in cities where the number of white children to mix with has shrunk to ludicrous proportions. And that has given rise to as yet unrecognized theories of so-called metropolitan desegregation. During the short-lived though greatly effective period of Title VI enforcement, from 1965 to about 1971, the federal administration also took this course.

I wonder, though, if we have not gone about as far as we are likely to get through the courts, which are themselves about the whitest institutions left in the South (no black has yet been appointed to a federal court; only one black yet sits on a state appellate court—Judge Morial, who holds an elected judgeship in New Orleans) and which have a very limited number of remedies they can use, busing being the most readily available. Archibald Cox put it well last year, in an address to the NAACP Legal Defense Fund:

But the power of the great constitutional decisions ultimately rests upon the Court's ability . . . to command a consensus. If the gap grows too wide—if the community is not persuaded to follow the law made by judges or if the feeble sanctions available to courts are not enough when added to the moral force of legitimacy—then the law will be changed, either by avowal or by lapse into desuetude. The aspirations voiced by the Court must be those the people are willing not only to avow but in the end to live by.

I speak these thoughts not as a counsel of judicial caution, but as a reminder that the struggle for human justice, while advanced by litigation, cannot be won by litigation only. In the end, equality must be achieved in the minds and hearts of people. The courts can lead in certain areas but they cannot indefinitely go it alone. If we value constitutionalism, we must persuade the people, therefore, to support the courts.

You have now, I understand, three counties where blacks control the school boards. There are other counties where population figures show that it could be, and many others where there is or could be sufficient voting power to establish strong influence within the school systems. I think this is the only sound way for moving farther along toward nondiscriminatory schools, schools serving as best we know how the children, the community, and the teachers. We might wish there was some easier, quicker way. There isn't. Not in Mississippi, not in Atlanta, not in Boston is the energy of lawyers within a courtroom a substitute for the energy of voters concerned to shape a school system to the best interests of their children as they see them.

When those SNCC and CORE workers came into Mississippi fourteen years ago, they came with a quiver full of hopes and dreams, and one of them they called "participatory democracy." I always thought that one was worth believing in, especially with institutions such as schools, which simply can't run well without free participation in their decision making by non-professionals and non-power holders, and by that I mean the participation of parents and students. It's at the polls, at school board meetings, and at public meetings that that participation can be secured and exercised, and those, not the courtrooms, are where, it seems to me, the resolution of the school issues of the late 1970s should occur. It is where there can be "participatory democracy" that there can be engaged the full, throbbing range of ideas of parents and students.

Joyce Ladner reported how surprisingly strong was the concern among teenage black girls for peace and for an end to international conflict; one of them said, with a wisdom that your Senators haven't—unless they are cynics—"as long as they are sending men to fight in Vietnam, we won't have any peace here."[2] We need to have schools that let this kind of thinking grow, wisdom that comes up from the people. It is to the great credit of the Mississippi Council that it has seen that the web of injustice is a seamless one, and thus you have taken your side—and the right side—on such issues as amnesty, the struggle of the Farmworkers' Union, and prison reform. These too are children's services, because they say to those young eyes watching you: This is what is required of you as free persons living in dignity.

Your model becomes a choice; they don't have to look only to that Congressional delegation, or to preachers who have lost sight of the prophetic tradition. We might all, for that matter, look at the words of the prophet Malachi, in the very last verse of the Old Testament: "And he will turn the hearts of fathers to their children and the hearts of children to their fathers, lest I come and smite the land with a curse." All of us were once children, and all who are children today will, all too soon, be, as we say, grown-up. We who are now older than they have made of this state, this South, this nation, this world whatever they have become, and we shall pass them on with their full freight of troubles, and also joys. The greatest gift we have in our power to give the children who will inherit this mixed legacy is the sense that life can be freer, that men and women can, if they will to do so, live at peace with each other and with nature, and that they can make this happen. By your example of stubborn labor for humane values and purposes, you are doing that for the children of Mississippi. You are offering them a sense both that a better and brighter life is possible and that they are not helpless. And while that prospect is kept alive before them, the children will grow well.

7

Remarks to the Southern Regional Council

1977

What is a revolution? At the very least, it results in a change of leaders or rulers. The civil rights movement hardly qualifies on that test because pretty much the same sorts still run things, though African Americans and Latinos did win some modest participation in rule. The great transformations which the nation has witnessed were produced by economic forces, including ones set loose by the civil rights accomplishments.

The revolt of African-American Southerners came about when they would no longer acquiesce in segregation. This revolt forced the nation to decide whether to impose a South African degree of force or to yield. Jim Crow, it used to be said, could not live without Uncle Tom, and he was dying. The second paragraph of my speech reprinted below alludes to present worldwide oppression of darker skin people. Can it be believed that they will peacefully accept that down the passageways of the twenty-first century? It will not be a calm century.

In the comments to the first selection of this book I said that the "New Negro" had been proclaimed as often as the "New South." Martin Luther King Jr. spoke at Bennett College in North Carolina of that "New Negro" only days after the end of the Montgomery boycott in an address now handsomely printed in the college's Social Justice Lecture Series:

> One day Jesus stood before a group of men of his generation, and I
> can imagine that they stood before the Master with that glittering eye,

wanting to hear some good. And Jesus looked at them and said in no uncertain terms, "I come not to bring peace but a sword." Jesus didn't mean he came to bring a physical sword. Neither did he mean that he did not come to bring true peace. But what Jesus was saying was this: That I come not to bring this old negative peace, which makes for deadening passivity and stagnant complacency. I come to bring positive peace, and whenever I come, a conflict is precipitated between the old and the new. Whenever I come, a division sets in between justice and injustice. Whenever I come, something happens between the forces of light and the forces of darkness. I come not to bring this old negative peace, which is merely the absence of tension, but I come to bring a positive peace, which is the presence of love and brotherhood and the kingdom of God. And the peace which Jesus talks about is always a positive peace.

So the peace which existed at this particular time in our nation was a negative peace devoid of any positive means. Then as the years unfolded, something happened to the Negro. Circumstances made it necessary for him to travel more. His rural plantation background gradually gave way to urban industrial life. His cultural life was gradually rising through the steady decline of crippling illiteracy, and even his economic life was rising through the growth of industry and the power of organized labor and other agencies.

All of these forces conjoined to cause the Negro to take a new look at himself. Negro masses all over began to reevaluate themselves, and the Negro came to feel that he was somebody. His religion revealed to him that God loves all of his children, and that all men are made in his image. He came to see that every man, from a bass black to a treble white is significant on God's keyboard. And so he could unconsciously cry out with the eloquent poet, "Fleecy locks and black complexion cannot forfeit nature's claim. Skin may differ, but affection dwells in black and white the same. Were I so tall as to reach the pole, or to grasp the ocean at its span, I must be measured by my soul. The mind is the standard of the man."

And with this new sense of dignity and this new self-respect, a new Negro came into being. And the tensions which we witness in the South today can be explained in part by the revolutionary change in the Negro's evaluation of his nation and destiny.[1]

In the closing months of the pre-atomic age, the Southern Regional Council was formed out of conviction that race was the central issue of the South. Though it may seem to us that nearly all else has changed during the hectic decades since, I doubt that race has yet yielded its place, though the problems it shapes and propels grow in their own various ways.

Nor has it yielded its place of primary importance elsewhere in the world. Even our own attention is, these days, more concentrated on the grim racial conflicts of southern Africa than on the still harsh relationships here. In truth, though, we can see that it is all one continuing struggle of mankind to free itself from a wrong turning it somehow made dark centuries ago, into the sadness, the sickness, the cruelty of racial pride. There have been political revolutions that, because they seemed to express noble ideals as well as partisan interests, have blazed outward all over the world. One thinks, principally, of the American, the French, and the Russian Revolutions of modern times. I expect generations to come may see the civil rights revolt as like them, may see it as America's second sending forth of impulses toward freedom to enchained peoples. I don't believe it is fanciful to see the road from Selma turning now toward Pretoria.

To say that is, of course, not to say that we stand on the edge of happiness. Twelve years after Selma we certainly haven't it here in satisfying measure, and in some important ways are, it now and then seems to me, worse off. I have worked and lived most of those years in the New York area, and as far as I can judge the conditions of black and Puerto Rican poor (and most blacks and Puerto Ricans are poor, or close to being so) have worsened by almost any measure one selects, whether it be political power, housing, employment, or schools. Indeed, when one considers what are, after all, the vast changes within the South, when one takes account of how the "black revolt" was a powerful and constructive example to our Mexican-American and Indian fellow citizens, when one sees and weighs all that and yet more too that came from the great movement and then looks at the conditions of the urban poor of the North, it is as if they almost alone sacrificed for the progress of others.

There have been other kinds of setbacks as well. We have traded in the perhaps impossible dreams of the sixties and accepted meaner ideals in return. And, saddest of all, the grave *has* had its victory. We lost Martin Luther King Jr., and George Wallace survives. We gave up Medgar Evers, but Jim Eastland will run again and likely win. Robert Kennedy was killed, and Richard Nixon ruled. Whitney Young and Audrey and

Stephen Currier drowned, but redlining bankers and self-protective foundation boards go on as before, controlling the money. George Wiley drowned too, and Daniel Patrick Moynihan prospered. Walter Reuther, that man who always wanted labor to connect with humanity's call, crashed to his death, while Frank Fitzsimmons, who wants only to connect with dollars, was becoming the single most powerful labor leader. These were crushing losses, and as yet unreplaced. There were others as well. Has any nation or cause ever lost so many of its natural leaders in such a short time?

Indeed, when we look back on the shining values of a dozen years ago and compare them with what that fine columnist Bill Raspberry has correctly called the "situation ethics" of contemporary politics,[2] what can we do but weep, or rage? What instructions about political morality are we supposed to receive when a month ago the Senate celebrated Messrs. Eastland and Stennis for their thirty years of joint membership in that body, three decades in which they have powerfully opposed just about any and every move toward human rights, justice for the weak, peace for the world. From the White House, Mr. Carter wished those men "many more years of dedicated service." Surrounded by capers and cutups like this, one can only wonder if we are supposed to take politics seriously. Are we all expected to fall into the game, chanting I'm okay, you're okay, Eastland and Stennis are okay, Helms is okay, Nixon too—the Vietnam War and all who made it—and especially those among its makers now called back to serve a Democratic president—they're okay too?

All of this in the name of political realism, but I no longer can believe in that. Somehow down those winding roads of so-called realism the poor, of this but also of foreign nations as well, always seem to stay poor, the wars and preparations for war ceaselessly plod on, and the owners of the world's and our nation's wealth go on owning it. John Lewis had it almost correct when, back in 1968 while still a staff member of the Southern Regional Council, he went once up to Vanderbilt and in a speech titled "Human Rights—A Final Appeal to the Church" pronounced "Woe unto the political leaders who listen to the voices of expediency and act in the interests of a Great Consensus, rather than do what is right."[3] *Almost* correct, because most of the woe, at least so far as we can see, falls not on the political leaders but on those they lead.

Let us confess, in honesty and fairness toward ourselves, that the ideals of the early sixties were perhaps too high and hard, that the hopes for non-violence and the "beloved community" lie beyond us. Let us accept that, let *that* be our "realism," even though any of you who share with me the good luck of knowing personally any of the heroes of South Africa, many of whom are now banned, will have to add that those same impossible ideals are moving people there as they once did here. Nevertheless, let us come down from the mountain, a bit. We do not need to come down so far.

The Southern Regional Council, along with the rest of the civil rights movement, has trusted in and practiced the methods of education, enlightened propaganda, political empowerment, and economic pressures of one kind or another. There have been at least two other methods, trusted in and used. Indeed, during the days of "massive resistance" in the 1950s they were the movement's principal methods in company with those lawyers who were realizing the American bar's highest moment before or since in courtrooms up and down the land. They were the methods of making friendships across the racial line and of, to use a recent term, consciousness raising. We need more of both today. It is too bad that the state and local councils on human relations have been allowed to decline. We need them, or their spirit, again, for the South is now as it was, a region where human relations, both bad and good but too often the former, weave the fabric of social life.

I have the feeling that there is, despite desegregation, almost less racial contact today than a decade ago. I have to admit that most of my own black friends are ones I've known for a long time, and I suspect that too many other liberals, black and white, might have to concede similarly on that point. We, black and white, need to learn again why we used to like each other. So let us not be wholly preoccupied with "doing"—let us give more time to "being" with each other and in each other's hopes and needs.

On the whole, I think the estrangement I sense is more the responsibility of blacks than whites, and the bridging of it will have to depend more on blacks. There is historical reason for that. At various points during the 1950s, it became clear that despite the loving and tireless effort of many good and some even great white Southerners, their leadership would not succeed. The reform of the South passed then to black leadership. The greatest of black leaders, Martin King, and others such as George Wiley, knew how important it was that black goals be seen, as in fact they are, linked with all those of democracy and peace. Their appeal was always to the nation as a whole, to fulfill *its* Constitution, *its* principles, to become in its own interest transformed. It is tempting today for black leaders, rightfully impatient with the pace of change, to address themselves not to the whole nation or even to its liberal elements, but just to its political and corporate leadership, to its so-called power structure, and to speak as race leaders, not as popular or national leaders. And that is what opponents of reform covertly or unconsciously welcome. For if unemployment, poor learning in the schools, or crime in the streets are allowed to be seen as *black* problems (or Puerto Rican or Chicano ones) they will likely never be solved, and their persistence year after year will only deepen and reconfirm all racial stereotypes in white minds. That is why one so fervently wishes that "summit" meetings of black leaders would not merely make demands on Congress and the White House, but would see themselves, as their predecessors of a decade ago did, as the reform leaders of this nation and would boldly claim the allegiance that is rightfully and historically theirs. Unemployment, bad schooling, and crime are not racial problems, no matter how many blacks or Hispanics may be trapped in them. They are national problems, residues of inequitable political and economic systems, and the responsibility of all of us. There is nothing I know of or can imagine in the history of our times to lead one to believe that political office holders or corporate executives—who more and more interchange with each other, just like all those football platoons—will do much about these very tough, very big, very real problems, and ones which are very much part and parcel of "our system," unless the sort of black and white multitude that demanded the reforms of 1964 and 1965 will again come into being.

It is time for black leadership to call upon white liberals to come back home. To do it, black leaders will have to accept the fact that today Hispanic leaders must stand beside them. And it must be done without rancor—the time for scapegoating "liberals" is past, if it ever was. There will have to be an effort made to understand liberal devotion to causes like peace, anti-militarism, the sanctity of the environment, and the dignity and aspirations of women. But it is time for liberals to come back to the cause they slipped away from, back to the unfinished business of equality—and it is time for black leadership to summon them. There has been enough knocking at the door of Washington and Wall Street. Those 50 percent black youth unemployment rates will go downward only when the kind of liberal mass that brought about the Civil Rights Act of 1964 and the Voting Rights Act of 1965 is made again to know what democracy requires of it.

Energies have not, of course, been dormant. Possibly never in our or any other nation's history have they so flourished—or, unhappily, have needed to. Those energies ended a wretched war in Vietnam, have thrown some hard punches at the CIA and the government's other lawless snoopers, have begun learning about and probing at the Pentagon, have thrown up weighty obstacles to industry's and consumers' ravages of the environment, have built countless and durable if small new community organizations, have fought for the rights of children, of mental patients and prisoners, of hungry people, and have given to women a new vision of themselves. And it all began in the heat of Mississippi and Alabama and Georgia and the rest of our South, just as was born here the impulse that has stirred Hispanics and Indians, and just as came from here the deeper resolve of people in southern Africa. And it all serves the same end, and, though that end may not be as holy a one as the "beloved community," it is a good and lovely one nonetheless of men and women living at peace with each other and with nature.

I I I

The South has had, as Vann Woodward put it, the burden of its own history. The South has also, of course, been a burden to the rest of the country. It still is, though [it is] becoming less of one. Its Senators and Representatives are almost never to be found at the forefront of good works. On the other hand, they are not, in anything like the degree they once were, barriers to the satisfaction of national needs. I have spent some time recently studying certain votes of this session of Congress, and I think what one can currently report is that the southern delegations are about as bad or as good as the rest of Congress, which is a milestone in the further Americanization of Dixie, no doubt helped along by a Georgian at the other end of Pennsylvania Avenue. There is no distinction among the Southerners, certainly no Estes Kefauver or Frank Graham, nor anymore a Sam Ervin, William Fulbright, or Lister Hill who, though terrible on civil rights, would partially atone by distinguished service in some other area. It is perhaps the age to which I've arrived, but all the world these days seems dominated by mediocre talents; in art, literature, science, philosophy, wherever, the days of genius or even brilliant sparkle seem gone, for a while. It would be too much to expect that Congress would rise above, or even up to the level of, that all-conquering modern mediocrity. And it does not.

If not generally worse than their colleagues, southern Congressmen and Congresswomen do still sometimes hear the old tribal drums. Southerners in the House voted better than 2–1 to build the B-1, even over Mr. Carter's opposition; but in the old days, not a third of them would have resisted the military. So one may take what consolation he can from that. The worst display of southern militarism came on the vote whereby Mr. Carter's all-too-modest program to upgrade the less-than-honorable discharges of Vietnam veterans (which in disproportionate numbers were of black and other minorities) was mean-spiritedly put down by the House by denial to them of all veterans' benefits. Only *one* Representative of those states that once had themselves been in rebellion, Fisher of Virginia, voted for compassionate justice for those many thousands of young victims of our war-making in Vietnam. One Vietnam veteran put the case exactly, though futilely, in a statement to a subcommittee of the House: "Those possessing bad discharges are already so burdened by unemployment, poverty, and lack of education that the benefits would have provided some new ray of hope to an otherwise dark future. One wonders why some Congressmen persist in policies that result in holding down those who are already at or near the bottom."[4] (Interestingly, although nearly all the rest of the "black caucus" were against this punitive bill, Representatives Ford and Jordan were not, choosing to stand with the southern bloc rather than the racial one. May they find a better issue the next time they do! To their credit, both of them did vote against the B-1, as did nearly all the rest of the "black caucus.")

On abortion, the Southerners in the House have, on the crucial issue of the use of Medicaid funds, stood about 5–4 against on the many votes that have been taken, a ratio no worse than the rest of the House (but one as good as it is only because of the astonishing support of the Carolina delegations). There have been so many votes taken on this issue this year that an exact picture of where legislators stand is hard to come by, but on the votes in the Senate that I have examined, Southerners are voting a consistent majority for the pro-abortion position.

If the tribal drums seem to be responded to less readily, the leading strings of economics seem about as tight as ever, all flighty talk of southern populism notwithstanding. Sixteen of the southern Senators voted, against Mr. Carter, to end price controls for newfound natural gas. A bill in the House to end federal farm subsidy payments to absentee corporations came within a surprising eight votes of passage, but only nineteen of its supporters were from the South. And so it goes. One could add more examples to the point that Southerners in Congress seldom fail to wait on the interests of big oil, big finance, big farms, and big money in general.

I have gone at this length into Congressional behavior for two reasons. One is to suggest to you that the South has a different political position in relation to the rest of the nation than it used to have. Southern blacks and white liberals used to look to Washington for indispensable help in solving our problems. That long-lasting period of political dependency is now so close to being over that we may as well call it finished. Now the South must play its full part in the resolution of national issues, and [it] has no excuse for not doing so.

Secondly, I wanted to suggest—and here I unashamedly speak as a liberal—that the South must play its part in the great liberal causes of our day. It was wrong, morally and politically unacceptable, for a Hill, Fulbright, or Ervin to be "good" on other issues, and reactionary on civil rights. It would be also wrong and unacceptable for a Southerner today to excuse his positions on war and peace and militarism, on secrecy and surveillance, on ecological necessities, on the economic rights of the poor, on the dignity of women, or on the claims of other minorities by doing a good turn here and there, or even many of them, for civil rights. When one hears of possible or actual support for an Eastland or Wallace or Thurmond, how dearly can one say the old dreams are valued?

I had an experience some years ago, in one of my first visits among Indians of the Southwest, which made me vividly realize something black friends had been gently and tactfully telling me also, and that I had not heard well. I sat with some Indians one day, and they began attacking me—*me!*—for policies and actions of the government in Washington. It struck me forcefully that they weren't distinguishing between me, the possibly somewhat prideful critic of politicians and bureaucrats, and those very fellows; all one, all pale face. I've come to accept this. I can accept the fact that to a black person, dealing with a white liberal may be only a variation of dealing with a white segregationist: all one, all white. It is beside the point, for the point is to build a society at peace with itself and other societies, to build a society within which all men and women and their children too can find decent and dignified lives. And in the service of that purpose we have all equal duties.

Our politics is throwing up men (e.g., Nixon and Agnew; you can add other, and many, examples) whose instincts are not for life and not for civilization, but for their destruction. Such men are a revolt against evolution. These are men who have the smell of death about them. But we are all infected with that plague, or else we would not elect and reelect such people. We lust for skill, we admire it and are infatuated with it, and we admire its possessors, those who can deal efficiently with the "system." But being smart in dealing with the "system" is small potatoes in this nuclear age. These men who govern us are the custodians of *life* itself, yours and mine and our families and friends and that of all people and of nature too.

Speaking about women, Erik Erikson once wrote that "True equality can only mean the right to be uniquely creative."[5] I believe the same can and must be said of blacks, of Hispanics and Indians, of white ethnics long cast down, must be said of Africa and Asia and Latin America as they come into the councils of nations. What America wants and what the world wants is not simply for new groups to share in its few privileges, but for those new folks to bring with them their own rich insights and understandings, for them to shape society to themselves and not they to it and its death-ridden ways.

Talk like that sounds more out of place today than it did when Baldwin said he didn't want to be integrated into a burning house. All

I can say is that I have little faith that the house won't burn unless those who, in our region and nation and world, are cut off from its power and riches find or create ways to make the economy and politics serve them—adapt to them—rather than be their suffocating embrace.

New ideas and values have more often than not come from "new" people—i.e., people newly emergent into social consequence. The world has no need for a "black political theory" or a "female" one either, nor for a "black" or a "female" theology, or lifestyle, or what have you. But it is likely, I believe, that the thinking which may give birth to sanity in our lives and culture will be bred, is being bred, in the experiences and insights of being black (or Hispanic, or Asian, or American Indian) or being woman.

❙ ❙ ❙

And so I conclude by speaking again to you as Southerners, and as one who wants still to think of himself as a Southerner, and to such, and as such, say that I don't like that bastard label "sunbelt." The sunbelt is, at best, nothing more than an expanse of land and sunshine, at worst a place replete with problems you don't need. To be a "sunbelter," if that's what it is called, is to be a rootless, non-historical person—and that, no matter what else, no proper Southerner can be. The South is not merely a geographical term. We are too far down the road of time for that. The South's identity, all that it has to offer, is a history, and a spirit dragged and wrenched from it. A spirit that, at its deepest, knows that life—mere life—is worth all, because it can come back another day and is, anyway, in the final judgment all we have, and knows that each of us has claims on each other that may be denied for long, but not forever. Let the burden of southern history be transformed now into the message of southern history. Let the South stand publicly for what it has since 1865 always stood privately: for life, for the tenacious holding on to it, and for the unavoidable sharing of it.

To some it may seem ironic that "human rights" became the government's announced foreign policy when a southern moderate became president. Let us now not stop to ponder causes for that, but only give thanks for the event while we closely and critically watch for its meaning and its carrying out. If that policy grows out of a truly southern understanding of the rightful needs of humanity, it will everywhere stand for the protection of life and the equal claims of all to it. And if so, the South would have turned the burden of its history into a lovely gift to our republic and to human kind.

8

The South: Then and Now

1978

As in the other speeches, this one mentions events and dates that are probably fuzzy in memories. Recalling them exactly is not important; their general significance will be apparent from the context, as will be the quarter-century-later similarities.

In 1978, I confessed puzzlement over how to interpret what the South had become and was becoming. The feeling has grown. Is there meaning left to that historical entity and culture we called the South? Maybe not.

Unfortunately, some old characteristics do continue in full measure: the South has too many poor and hurting people and is the nation's seedbed of militarism. And the southern political and economic structure has proved capable of admitting new persons—African Americans mostly—without changing its essential nature.

I have puzzled long, too long and fretfully perhaps, over what to say today, and the tone in which to cast it. I wish I could promise, or even slyly hint to you, that out of all that puzzling has come something valuable and usable by you, but I can't; I am not characteristically a self-deprecating man but the bare truth is that I don't know how to put into words my sense, my intuition, about these days we're living. I have been asked to speak on the topic, "The South: Then and Now" and I feel much more sure of what it was in the past than of what it is now.

It is not that analysis or even prediction are all that hard; they are, unfortunately, often all too easy. If you predict, as I usually do, on the pessimistic side, the percentages work in your favor, and do so more and more as these years of the late Twentieth Century go by. When I read each morning's newspaper, I have a daily impulse to run for cover.

But today's should be a happy occasion, as we celebrate Elridge [McMillan] and John [Griffin]. Indeed, that may point to the meaning we ought to hold before ourselves, and keep coming back to, that even in the midst of political madness what still counts, and what mysteriously appears and reappears, is the individual, whose very self is a celebration of life, and a rediscovering of it, generation after generation. That, at least, we did learn from being Southerners, had that truth beautifully—and powerfully—expressed for us by our great novelists, by our deep and lovely spirituals and by our haunting folk, and country music.

One of those old civil rights movement songs, not as well known as some others, goes, "They say that freedom is a constant struggle," and then follow other refrains: "They say that freedom is a constant marching"; and "constant dying"; and so forth. I was in a gathering a fortnight or so ago where one of the old SNCC guitarists and singers led us in that song. He ended with a stanza I didn't remember hearing before: "They say that freedom is a constant loving."

Freedom is a constant loving.

Happenings like that are forever trapping me. I go my pessimistic way, being nearly always right, and then get jolted by a song (or by a suddenly star filled sky or an early air of Spring) once again into a hope that individuals—I'm never jolted high enough to have hope again for governments—may yet find their way to peace and freedom.

So one looks for the words and tone with which to express that, to voice a hard, battle toughened hope amidst numbing despair over national and world politics. I look, but I caution you, I only doubtfully find. One looks especially hard because not only do we celebrate John and Elridge but, as southern liberals always do when they congregate, we celebrate ourselves. We meet here in a gracious hotel called "Colony Square," but wherever *you* are assembled is no colony. It's liberated territory; and not very square either. Yet one of the clarion calls you followed in that civil rights movement which offered liberation to the South—non-violence—is little honored anywhere today; and the other great message of those days—the passion for equality—seems dimmer day by day.

So we had our victory, a triumph won for the South not by its politicians or businessmen but by those whom John Ehle in his fine book by the same name called "the free men"[1]; free women too, as Ehle's text if not his title made clear. Possibly where things began to go wrong was when those free men and women who had struggled, marched, loved, and—yes—died some of them, were not, except for a few, called on to finish the job. It was an amazing thing. The *free* people won a revolution down here, and, lo and behold: the same *other* people— or their political twins—stayed in political power, continued to rule. Some good local and legislative offices have been won by blacks, and even by a white liberal or two (and that of course never happened *then*, and I am here to talk about the "then and now"), but beside them we have still the familiar roster of names and types. Look, for example, at the Senators the South still sends to Washington. What a depressing crew they are, most all of them.

Is there any among them who cares for non-violence and equality?

We again read in the newspapers that "populists" are charging to the fore in southern politics. This is, possibly, good news, though I haven't yet read of anyone being elected to state-wide office in Texas or Louisiana disliked by oil, in the Carolinas opposed by textiles or tobacco, in Kentucky or Virginia or West Virginia against the pleasure of coal, or in Georgia against the wishes of Coca-Cola, and all that.

But whether populists or folks in gray flannel suits go to the state capitals and to Washington, whether blacks or whites, women or men, this country has some problems left over from the days of the civil rights movement. Here are four of them.

Schools Once we struggled to desegregate schools. Now the largest issue is the future of public schools, for increasingly there seem to be hardly any city people who send their children, black or white, to the public schools of the inner city, if they have a realistic alternative, either of private or suburban public schools.

War and Militarism   The Vietnam war stopped the "war on poverty" in its tracks. Now a military budget bigger than the one we had then and growing every year keeps it stopped. The single most depressing event of the past year or so was Mr. Carter's Wake Forest address, where, in words that marched in perfect step with those of his four predecessors, he formally committed his presidency to the same arms race, the same interventionist and expansionist foreign policies that are rendering the life of this earth and its people "poor, nasty, brutish," and probably short.

Law Enforcement   Another book written about those passionate 1960s was called *Southern Justice*.[2] In it, a number of lawyers told of their experiences with southern police, sheriffs, jailors, prosecutors, judges, and juries. One of the great deeds of the civil rights movement, I think its greatest, was to change that. The movement ended fear. It took away from the white South its cruelest weapon, the ability to terrorize. The last year or so has, however, shown signs that the South may have exported "southern justice" not only to northern city governments, like Philadelphia's, but to Washington and the national government as well. The Department of Justice has displayed an hostility to civil liberties which has equaled if not surpassed the misconduct of the Department during Mr. Nixon's years. It has defended with incredible tenacity the wrongful practices of its predecessors, even to the degree, in a scandalous instance, of asserting that it might not obey the Supreme Court if ordered by it to divulge identities of its informers on the Socialist Workers Party. The Department has also publicly stated that it had television surveillance on a person, in part to assert the president's inherent power to do so without a warrant. It is prosecuting Frank Sneppes for his book on the CIA's blunders, pettishly seeking to confiscate his earnings from it. The Department has practiced what looks remarkably like selective and preferential prosecuting policies, indicting Mr. Kearney but not his superiors in the FBI; indicting two officials of International Telephone and Telegraph for lying about the Company's role in fomenting armed revolution in Chile but not their boss; extending to Mr. Helms a bargain that he could say he would wear as a badge of honor. We have seen the nigh-unbelievable spectacle of the Department taking before the Supreme Court the position that a Congressional aide who committed burglary *or even murder* in the line of work could not be prosecuted or sued. I could, sadly, go on. It is a record of disgrace, and if it represents a southern view of justice we shall have heavy and hard days ahead.

Poverty The 1963 "march on Washington" was for "jobs and freedom," but unemployment today is greater than it was then. Between 1967 and 1977, the black unemployment rate rose, according to the National Urban League, from 7.4% to 13.2%.

I don't want to be or seem to be disparaging. This is a far different South and nation than twenty years ago, and a better one too. Twenty years ago (1957–58) we had a South where in Arkansas 91 black youngsters were in school with whites, 11 were in North Carolina, 19 in Tennessee—and that except for west Texas was it. Twenty and even 15 years ago we had a South where everything was segregated and unequal, from, for example, the drinking fountains that provided white and colored water to the municipal swimming pools that more often than not, like so many other things, had only white. Even 15 years ago, no such meeting as this could be held here in downtown Atlanta. Twenty years ago there were no more than 1 1/4 million registered black voters across the eleven state South, and that was probably an over-estimate. We had about 30 counties with heavy black populations where not a single black was permitted to vote. There were virtually no black office holders. Less than 20 years ago the South's state universities were still rigidly segregated (as were most of its private ones too) and the battles—and they literally were that—of Oxford, Tuscaloosa, and Athens lay ahead. Twenty years ago—and even 12 or 13 years ago—southern police and sheriffs and courts still carried out that role they had been assigned by southern society since slavery days, that of keeping the Negroes controlled and in their place, by whatever means they saw fit. Twenty years ago, and indeed only 10 years ago or less, hunger—plain, uncomplicated hunger and malnutrition—was commonplace.

This has all been changed, and it was *you* and people like you who did it. You—not your Confederate ancestors, if you had those—but *you* are the finest people the South has ever produced, because it was *you* who slew the dragon. Don't forget that you did that. Don't belittle what you did. Don't, above all, lose your self-confidence; because you need it, and the nation needs you to have it.

For the thought I'd like to suggest to you is that when those free men and women—some of whom, of course, were your own younger selves—offered us liberation from colonial status, we didn't take it then; and now, for the sake of this country and humanity, we should claim it. I'd like to invite you to think of all the battles of the 50s and 60s, against segregation and discrimination and brutality, as being engagements that had to be fought and won on the way to the enemy's heartland. For the enemy is war and poverty and ignorance. We could never reach them before. We were ensnared, confused, tormented, and set at cross-purposes by race and sex and sectional pride—all barriers to our common humanity. We are a freer people now; free to contend at the core.

Let me suggest another thought to you. It is possible to visualize American history during the last century as characteristically a two-sided affair, one side being the growth of power and the other side being the peoples' adjustments to power. The power side of that picture has been almost wholly composed of two forces, each served by a thriving science and technology. These two forces are the corporations, incessantly growing to dominate the economy; and the national state, growing since the time of the Spanish-American War to become an almost independent existence, with interests of its own to protect, at home and all over the world, in the name of national security.

The other side, the people's adjustments to power, has been made up of countless individual acts and choices, but also of a succession of reform movements. Typically, and naturally, these many reform movements of the late 19th and 20th centuries were targeted on corporate and state power, though between World War II and the Vietnam War it was made out that to criticize or oppose state power was to be unpatriotic.

Some other developments, however, came along within American reform. One was the "prohibition" campaign, which happily went as well as came. Another was the women's suffrage drive of the teens, which reappeared during the last decade as a demand for women's rights and dignity. And most important of all as yet, there came the civil rights movement. For a decade and more, American reformers turned their attention almost solely to it. It was a glorious cause, but I submit to you that while, as it were, our backs were turned, corporate and state power grew as they had never grown before. Never had there been a magnification of the corporation and of the national security apparatus to rival what occurred in the 1950s and the 1960s.

Then, 20, even 10 years ago, our task was to secure rights, dignity, and breathing space for all people. *Now*, our task as a free people is to bring power to heel.

The southern experience of the past two or three decades is one of the great, if not the greatest, transformations in American history. One way of summarizing it all is to say that during these years the South moved into the present. It had never before lived in the present. White Southerners were always looking back to the past, for some meaning to their lives; and forward to the future for some hope. They had so boxed themselves in ideologically and politically that only the rare white could find either meaning or hope in the present. The present was not much good for anything except play, and play for some of the "good old boys" became a dreadful thing. Black Southerners played too in the present. They worked in it also, worked hard, but did so to escape from the present, to flee from a past of misery and pain, to reach out and find a future which supplied for them both the hope and the meaning of their lives.

Now, the South lives in the present, whether all like it or not. James McBride Dabbs, mentor to so many of us, said better, and more bluntly, what I have tried to convey. He used an image not of time but of place; specifically, the piazza. Listen to Dabbs:

> We make a great show of our personal relationships, but these are largely the froth of sociability; as to our intimate personal life, we are often like the old aristocrat, Major Buchan, of Allen Tate's *The Fathers*, who, when interrogated by a young acquaintance, "Sir, may I ask you a personal question?" thunders, "Sir, you may not!" The trouble here is not that the personal life of the Southerner is too deep to be expressed, it is rather too shallow for him to trust it. The Major would have said that his personal life lay between himself and

his conscience, or himself and God; but what he sensed was that it lay on the edge of the abyss, and one had better avoid the abyss.

Considered in this respect, southern culture [Dabbs was writing this in 1969] is a piazza [or porch] culture. . . . We built piazzas because the weather suggested it. . . . [We] became piazza people. Ideally, the piazza is a half-way point between the entirely private world protected by the walls of the home, and the entirely public world stretching away on all sides. Ideally, piazza people should possess the strength gained from years of deep companionship within the home and the ease and *savoir-faire* of men of the world. Ideally, they should have a religion to support their culture, and a culture to soften and humanize their religion. But the South, having built its material world upon a basic and ever more flagrant injustice, could not find real support for this world within the deep privacies of its being. It therefore avoided these deep privacies and heightened the laughter on the piazza in order to hide the vacancy within. In such a world, so purposefully social, asking a personal question became a threat rather than an invitation to human sharing, and "Sir, you may not!" thunders the Major.[3]

In all of this, Dabbs was, as is evident, talking about the white South and Southerners. He extended his thought to embrace Negro Southerners, but he like Faulkner was never really half so perceptive and insightful with them as with the whites they knew in their very marrow. Indeed, it some time ago came to seem to me that neither black nor white Southerners knew each other really so well as they claim to do. They knew how to make use of each other, and to hide from each other, and sometimes life would throw black and white individuals together in shared suffering; but that was and probably is about it. Quite possibly, none of us penetrates very well the mind and heart of another. Emerson said that two persons are like globes, which can touch each other only at a point. Sometimes I think he was wrong in saying that; but then again I'm not sure, and imagine he may have been right.

Black people were piazza people too, all over the South. Whites sat on those porches, keeping an arms length away from both the public world which seemed so meaningless, and the private world they feared. Maybe it has been the same with black people. Maybe to get away from the unbearable tension and artificiality of those piazzas was what led the most restless, the most hurt and provoked, of both races to flee off to the North.

What Southerners today, black or white, can believe in the North in that old way? We live now in the present. The termites and tornadoes have got to those piazzas; anyway, they don't build them on ranch-style houses in the new subdivisions, or on public housing. *Now*, it seems to me as I visit the South, that many Southerners, people like you, are seeking to integrate personal and public values without suppressing either, are seeking to integrate regional and national and even international responsibilities without neglecting either.

Others of us—and perhaps they are the most numerous—have raced into the present bent on out-hustling and out-consuming anybody and everybody. And we do all enjoy the nice hotels and restaurants and stores they have provided us. Sometimes it appears, though, that the suffering of Albany, Birmingham, Selma, New Orleans, Bogalusa, St. Augustine, Danville, Orangeburg, Monroe, Little Rock, Clinton, and Mississippi only freed the South to become the nation's new style Yankee peddler. If all the storm and pain and human dedication of the long years of distinctively southern history end with a race of managers and problem solvers, with little or no sense of purpose or values, sent off by a prideful people to executive suites and Washington offices, if all that that history lastingly taught was a veneer of southern manners and a fondness for southern cooking, it does seem somehow unfulfilled. Or, as some might say, unredeemed.

Recently I was reading again Ralph Waldo Emerson, and there suddenly flashed through my head the realization that his awesome essay on "Self-Reliance" had had at least one southern exemplar: the one that struck my memory was Richard Wright's *Black Boy*. Listen to Emerson, the deeply and widely educated Yankee:

> Whoso would be a man, must be a non-conformist. . . . Nothing is at last sacred but the integrity of your own mind.

Listen now to Wright, looking back on a miserably impoverished, ill-educated Deep South boyhood:

> It was inconceivable to me that one should surrender to what seemed wrong, and most of the people I had met seemed wrong. Ought one

to surrender to authority even if one believed that authority was wrong? If the answer was yes, then I knew that I would always be wrong, because I could never do it.

Listen again to the New England sage, this time from his essay, "Experience":

> Into every intelligence there is a door which is never closed, through which the creator passes.

Listen to Wright, puzzling over how it happened that he, unlike so many others, had not been crushed by what the Deep South did to him:

> The face of the South that I had known was hostile and forbidding, and yet out of all the conflicts and the curses, the blows and the anger, the tensions and the terror, I had somehow gotten the idea that life could be different, could be lived in a fuller and richer manner.

How do we, in fact, account for such a one as Wright? He came out of wretched poverty, had neither books nor teachers, had no father to speak of. A social misfit from the beginning, he scrapped and fought with everyone: family, churches, schools, neighbors. Indeed, the reader gets a sense of young Wright having to fight his way through, win his freedom of action from, the black community in order to get to the point where he could confront the white society, which he had known from his youngest years was his real enemy. It was somewhat as I earlier suggested to you may have been the deeper purpose of the civil rights movement itself, a freeing of ourselves to confront the real enemies, militarism and poverty.

Yet somehow, through amazing grace perhaps, Richard Wright made of this unlikely material a self, put together a self-reliant person. His way to that led through reading and books, and the books he read seem mainly to have been by white writers, novelists mostly, though the writer who first shoved him into an unappeasable desire for study and learning was the essayist H. L. Mencken, a man who might accurately be described as a racist. Even earlier, he assuaged his appetite for words with a weekly "KKK" tabloid, the only reading he could find. Wright was ready to explore whatever was offered, seeking what he could use. His way toward confrontation with the dominant white society led him to go North—taking, as he said, "a part of the South to transplant in alien soil to see if it could grow differently"—and in doing that he was like so many talented blacks then; and like so many talented whites, too.

What is different *now*, ladies and gentlemen, is that the South is habitable. The 1950s and 1960s may not have brought us to Canaan-land, but—and this was and is a great thing—they made it possible and inviting for the best of young Southerners, black and white, to stay at home and to work here.

What will they do, what will they work at? I don't know. I've already said that too many seem intent only on showing they can out-hustle anybody, anywhere. But I do believe that still alive and throbbing in the South is the same spirit that Richard Wright found in himself and which he described as "a sense of the world that was mine and mine alone, . . . that gave me insight into the suffering of others, . . . that [kept] alive in me the enthralling sense of wonder and awe in the face of the drama of human feeling which is hidden by the external drama of life."

And this is a good place for me to stop, standing with him in wonder before the drama of individual human feelings, despite the external, and usually saddening, life around them; for this is where I began, celebrating Elridge and John, and the many others of you who, come hell or high water, come principalities and power, come think-tanks and smoke filled rooms, come Wall Street and Pennsylvania Avenue, will go on working to make this life fit for humankind. You will do so as Southerners because everybody has to be somebody and you cannot be and would not want to be other than Southerners, men and women, black and white, living and working with each other in more equality than blacks and whites, women and men, ever shared before: and *that* you did, you brought *that* about. You, with a little help from your friends, have in fact done so well and gone so far at overcoming those ancient barriers of discrimination and separation that there will shortly be no excuse for our not going on to the main fray, to humanity's long postponed rendezvous with the evils of war-making and poverty. And though the odds may be against success, can we believe, can we afford not to believe, that there too we shall overcome?

9

Excerpts from *Minority Report*

1987

In the days of the August 2001 Durban conference on racism, lament was widespread over opportunity lost because the conference became beset with bitter political controversies. I did not see it that way. Conferences are seldom productive of new policy or even much action, but I wondered if this one may not have yielded more good than most. Western and certain of the Asian and African states wanted to debate along differing lines. There cannot ever be useful discussion when the terms of discussion and their definitions are imposed by one side. The conference illustrated how far apart are controlling concerns and perspectives.

Bayard Rustin almost alone among us in the 1960s and 1970s used to decry the term "racism." We cannot move ahead if we insist on wading through that swamp was essentially what he would tell us. Whether he ever wrote that, I don't recall, but I do well remember his sorrowing comments about the Kerner Report and its famed concept of two nations. Nothing positive can come of that, he argued: let's talk about specific economic and other goals we need to move on. I have not always adhered to that rule, but it is a valid one.

Disagreement in Durban was one necessary lesson. The desperate minds that caused the New York and Pentagon horror of September 11, 2001, were another. The street protests that have surrounded and tormented meetings of global financial leaders are yet another. Are they all perhaps sending the same message, that when so much *overwhelming power is concentrated in a few hands there is no other way to resist?*

> *Nature hath made men so equal... the weakest has strength enough to kill the strongest, either by secret machination or by confederacy with others that are in the same danger with himself. ... From this equality of ability ariseth equality of hope in the attaining of our ends.*

The words are Thomas Hobbes's (Leviathan, chapter 13), and none, especially not rulers of states, should ever forget them.

When I first put together this collection it had included nothing from the 1980s. The publisher questioned why, and in part I responded that I don't like the 1980s. That will be apparent in this piece, which we did finally select. The Reagan-Bush years were a time when the arrogance we inherited from the British became full-blown conceit: we felt ourselves to be our own sufficient standard of right, wherever in the world our perceived interests lay, and within our own land self-interest was held the acceptable test of morality. We progressively rendered our nation unfit for coping with or understanding the needs and values of weaker peoples. And, as many have said before me, they have as a result learned to hate us.

I truly believe that the only political alternative to social terror is law. And so, as an American, I am ashamed and angry when our government obstructs the spread of international law. It was Hobbes too who laid down that "Where there is no common power, there is no law: where no law, no injustice." (Leviathan, chapter 13) How is law to be established where there is no present law? The course of our civil rights movement may be instructive, even within the larger context.

The old South was a society grounded on terror. Behind every facet of gentility stood the terrorist. That society was reduced—overcome, we hope—by two forces. One was popular uprising; the other was law.

Law could impose itself on the terror-plagued South because in time the national Constitution came to be accepted, and that same Constitution—having become an instrument of reform—would protect the black uprising. I wish that present-day global reformers would fully recognize this and would concentrate their energies on creating and strengthening—and usually that will have to be against the opposition of our Congress and President—international institutions that could establish a framework of law within which justice for the weak can be effectively defined and defended. Without such institutional support lesser measures—apologies, reparations, and so forth—seem to me to promise little of lasting benefit.

And as law protected protest during our civil rights movement, so it had itself been engendered and given purpose by the life of that great arousal. The movement, from its ranks of great black leaders and equally great followers—mostly black but whites too—spoke from deep moral and religious convictions. I think these protests against "globalism" will have to find that kind of faith. Nations today, including our own, churn about on tides of technology and ideology. Their people will have to supply what neither of those nonhuman, and too often antihuman, forces can.

The selection that follows contains data that are old, but I think its essential conclusions still pertain. Inequalities still abound and oppress the less strong racial and ethnic groups. These inequalities show signs of growth and fewer signs of a large diminishing. There will be only occasional and fleeting peace while such is so—at home or abroad.

Poverty poses three sorts of problems for American policy. First and basic, what rank, what degree of importance, do we give to it; second, how do we define government's degree of responsibility for remedy; and third, what solutions do we shape, assuming we have not concluded that only the poor themselves are responsible for their own condition.

Until the nineteenth century, poverty was hardly even a topic in political theory. In the wake of the French Revolution, one after another writer turned to it, leading to the work of Marx and of the Fabians and English idealists late in the century (of whom the best representative was T.H. Green). Marx can be said to have proposed that poverty, or at least its cause, is the central issue of political philosophy, displacing its typical concern for political relationships and rights. The English writers are less well known to us, but practically meant a great deal more to us than did Marx, even if they had nothing like his seismic force. As John Rawls's book, *A Theory of Justice*, can be described as a justifying statement of American centrist liberalism, so Green's

Lectures on the Principles of Political Obligation a century before set its directions (and the fact that one writes as a social contractarian and the other wrote from a divergent stimulus does not affect the case).

Politics, Green held, must aid (or else, because it inevitably affects, will distort) the moral development of the members of a society. Its special role is the "removal of obstacles" to self-realization. Green adopted as the measure and criterion of social progress the erasure of barriers separating men from each other (e.g., slavery), thus making possible an ever-widening human fellowship. On this view, the recognition of rights belonging to man *as* man becomes the first mark of historical advance. The end is, however, the perfection of character, and as long as men are merely free from restraints their advance has been only "negative," although necessary. Ethical progress is completed when men in their freedom accomplish moral ends they have imposed on themselves. The free man is thus the emancipated man only in the first step; he is the emancipated man possessed of sufficient education, material means, and social status in the second step; the free man is, finally, the good man. That second step is "positive freedom." It is the purpose and domain of government. Negative rights, Green concluded, make inevitable positive freedom, because the former once acknowledged lead to effective demands for the latter, and because it is socially necessary that all who are politically responsible shall be politically capable. Positive freedom in turn makes possible the fuller development of the negative rights which, as they appertain to the spirit of man, are in the end more important. But it is hypocrisy, Green said, to speak of men as free as long as they remain fettered by ignorance, poverty, or—he added—alcohol. State power has the function of removing such obstacles to the development of self-reliant citizens and persons.

With variations of rhetoric and tone, that was essentially the program of British liberalism prior to 1945 and of the "welfare state" if not nationalization policies of the 1945–1951 Attlee government; of Wilson's "new freedom" and the Progressive movement; and of the Rooseveltian New Deal. All had an unself-conscious moral tone, which has been almost totally missing from post–World War II American political programs except for a brief revival in the 1964–1966 interlude of Johnson's administration. All aimed at enabling citizens to stand on their own feet. All saw the government's role as primarily the "removal of obstacles" through care for the economic security and education of the people. *None* saw poverty as necessary and acceptable, as a condition government could leave to market forces, as the Reagan administration does. As Rawls has written:

> What is just and unjust is the way that institutions deal with [unequal talents and social advantages] . . . there is no necessity for men to resign themselves to these contingencies. The social system is not an unchangeable order beyond human control but a pattern of human action. In justice as fairness men agree to share one another's fate.[1]

To return to our questions, the first—what political priority attaches to the problem of poverty?—has to be answered to the effect that none is higher. Men have debated for centuries the relative values of liberty, equality, order, and justice. There is a large and welcome measure of redundancy among them. There may, nevertheless, be enough distinction to make useful gradations of emphasis among them within a consensual society; i.e., within one where all who are legally held responsible for their acts may be fairly said to have given consent to those laws. But a permanently impoverished class cannot be said to have done so. Our steadily increasing prison population is tacit acknowledgment of this. For a republican society with a huge underclass, there is no feasible course consistent with professed principles and its own stability but to address the problem of poverty, and not turn from it.

From numerous sources the public hears that past governmental antipoverty programs have "failed," and that therefore, none should again be tried. Besides being flawed logic, the conclusion has few analogues in other areas of policy. What ever does work, once and for all? Our foreign policies, based on suspicion of the Soviet Union, have not reduced the USSR's influence or power; they have instead led us into seemingly endless military involvements abroad and have imposed upon us incredibly large expenditures. Yet their failure to achieve their goal—the reduction of Soviet power—is not seen by either Democratic or Republican leadership as a cause for change. Our farm policies have achieved only one of their proclaimed goals—the increase of production. They have failed miserably at any of the others, such as protection of the "family farm" or a better life for rural people, who have instead been propelled in droves by those policies to the slums of the cities. Yet we continue in them, with mere shifts of emphasis. Our policies to reduce use of narcotics have not worked; should we now encourage narcotic use? Goals deemed essential by government are pursued. The abolition of persistent poverty is essential. Hardly anyone publicly denies that. But adequately funded and, above all, sustained policies toward that goal do not follow.

Our policy fluctuations, from one administration to another, are like those in foreign policies: neither affects the larger prevailing patterns of our political economy, which are capitalism and Soviet rivalry. This is not to say that changes of administrations do not matter. They do, often intensely so, as they bring about variations of methods and tactics, of sensitivity to suffering and hardship, and of understanding of rights and liberties. Often these quite important variations revolve about, in terribly damaging ways, our attitudes and acts toward the weak, toward the poor at home and the poorer nations abroad. At home, changes of administration tend to register on a scale of harsher to milder forms of "trickle-down" theories. There have been no end to these, from Charles Wilson's "what is good for General Motors is good for the United States" to John Kennedy's "rising tide that lifts all boats" to Ronald Reagan's "supply-side economics." Without arguing economic merits, the common factor among them all is the subordination of the interests of the poor to other economic goals. Even if that were economically defensible, it is politically wrong.

Our second question—what is government's responsibility?—virtually is answered above. Poverty in industrial societies is a function of low income, and that is the result of unemployment or underemployment more than anything else. By 1983, the officially defined poverty rate included 15 percent of the population, which means nearly 35 million people; and unemployment hovered around 10 percent of the work force, double that for minorities, quadruple that for minority youth. The figures fluctuate from one reporting period to another. They nevertheless creep steadily upward. The causes have been well agreed upon: technological changes that have reduced the number of entry-level, unskilled jobs and have eliminated others through increased productivity; the particular case of agriculture, become now so thoroughly a capital-intensive industry that the farms have been amazingly depopulated; the transference of much labor-intensive manufacturing to foreign countries; the baby boom of the 1950s and 1960s, which has not been fully caught up with by the job market; the great increase in numbers of women in job competition with males; and a hard to measure but certainly large influx of immigrants in the 1970s from Latin America and Asia. These developments have represented *basic*—not transient—alterations of the economy. All or nearly all have arisen with the encouragement, express or tacit, of public policy, especially including tax policies. The first rule of personal morality is to accept responsibility for the consequences of one's acts; the rule of political morality should be little different. The poverty these governmentally encouraged or tolerated changes have caused requires a public response.

Today's poverty is not something done to the poor. It is not caused by policies—slavery or the old British enclosures would have been early examples of such, South African labor laws a contemporary one—framed deliberately to take advantage of the poor, as desired and as power allowed. Some of it, however, results from policies—not introduced by the Reagan administration but gaily carried further by it—to reward the rich. Today's poverty is caused by the way the economy works. Those workings make problems not only for the poor. The poor have less defense, however, nor do they share at all proportionately in the advantages and opportunities that these basic changes also produce; consequently, the gap between the poor and the mainstream widens. Nor, finally, is there much precedent for believing that the approaches society takes and will take toward smoothing out the problems spawned for it by basic changes (rebuilding American industry plans, for example) will have the fortunes of the poor much at heart or in mind; they will be left to the rising tide, though justice would require that they not be.

The third question—effective solutions—is hard; there can be no dispute about that, at least. Among the possible answers to it can be that government allow the market to solve the problem. That flies in the face of all experience, and all the judgments of the economic and political managers of other countries, but theoretically—and in this case contemporary American electoral politics bends today toward theory, toward ideology, and away from experience—it may be possible.

A more realistic approach is along a line already opened, that of entitlement. The American poverty problem, the seemingly pathological one that will not yield even to upward trends of the general economy, consists primarily of the millions among us for whom the economy has no apparent need: untrained or ill-trained, socially disoriented, culturally misfit, a very large proportion of them young blacks and Hispanics, many who are mothers without mates, many the children of single-parent households.[2]

Their situation is made more desperate by other complicating factors. First, just above them are millions who are employed at unskilled, low-paying jobs, many in such occupations as fast-food clerks, hotel workers, or other like segments of the expanding so-called "service industries," and who represent almost the only realistic jobs available to those below them. These are jobs that require little or no preliminary training, and consequently provide scant incentive for schooling or special training. A second factor is the large number today of the cyclically unemployed, people who do have skills and are attractive employees, and who compete for such jobs as become available, letting employers choose between hiring them or the perhaps less demanding and more tractable unskilled. A third factor is the ease of entry into and the low risks of the underground economy of drugs, gambling, and sex. A fourth factor is that the system of welfare, including food and medical assistance, does all but guarantee subsistence.

The welfare system is based on entitlement: if stipulated conditions are met, benefits are paid. Those conditions relate to income levels. Other entitlement programs have other criteria: veteran's status, disability, old age, unemployment compensation, etc. So well established and popular are these non-means-tested entitlements that they can be considered now part of the American plan of governing. The means-tested entitlements, on the other hand, become more or less generous as the political winds shift. Their purpose being nothing more than subsistence, the shift is mainly in the levels of poverty included as deserving of this "safety net," more or fewer, rather than in the size of subsistence provision for those included. The welfare system has no relevance to the ending of poverty; people don't get off welfare, or the need for it, by being on it. At best, it is a bureaucratically, sometimes degradingly, administered and minimally adequate support for those who really cannot work, or a "tiding over" for those out of work. For many, it operates in ways that actually discourage attempts to work, and becomes virtually a permanent arrangement. It is the price America pays to prevent noisome starvation and riotous protest. There are, moreover, many rural and urban communities in our poverty belts where the various forms of welfare—AFDC, Medicaid, food stamps, black lung compensation, etc.—are the principal economic base for everyone in the area, not just the poor.

But however poorly applied, the entitlement principle is a good one. It is also as close as the United States has come to the adoption of "positive rights." The principle could (and should) be extended further, beyond simple subsistence (and essentially that is also what old-age insurance and unemployment compensation are) to cover those things related to making an individual self-sustaining. Such has been the purpose of that largest of entitlement programs, the public school system. The indicated step beyond that is to make job training and entry-level, non-dead-end public service jobs available *as a right*. Mothers who cannot work because of children at home could have the supports they need, either to study at home or have day care provided. And as public schools are compulsory, so should be training and work, of some useful kind, by those not disabled. Between a permanent underclass and the availability of useful work, there is only doubtfully stable middle ground.

The entitlement principle does, in fact, already pervade all the relationships governments, state as well as federal, have toward the economy. Ours is an ideological politics in theory (the ideology of "free enterprise") but determinedly nonideological in application (unless, which may well be the case, the controlling if unstated ideology is simply the protection of vested interests). In recent years we have seen an intellectual revival of "free market" economics, and about it there is a beguiling persuasiveness. Many of us can recall how neatly and ineluctably the demand and supply curves intersected and balanced in our Economics I class, and the blackboard logic of them captures our sometime acquiescence still. The Reagan administration professes its faith in them, and when not inconvenient to its supporters' interests—more to the point, when convenient to its supporters' interests—follows them. In universities, think tanks, and some editorial pages a flock of writers has of late proclaimed them. The classical revival has included, to the good luck of its publicity, some black economists, notably Thomas Sowell and Walter E. Williams, whose prescriptions for ending black poverty consist chiefly of abolishing the minimum wage and curtailing, if not undoing, the strength of labor unions.[3]

Perhaps—who knows?—with a clean slate, free-flowing demand and supply could work. In the tight interlock between politics and economics that history has fashioned the doctrine is meaningless. The American economy long ago claimed the American political system as its own, and has managed it more than it has been managed. The political aims of business are not and have not been primarily derived from creed, but from insistence that Washington and state capitals recognize and observe the *specific* interests of *specific* segments of the business system. The oil industry, the banks, the media, the wheat growers, and all the rest *each* have their welcome in and access to governing circles; and political decisions are made within the context of accommodating their interests, as they each have defined them. In short, they have insisted upon their *entitlements*.[4]

It is an imperfect but not necessarily bad political economy. It resembles and, indeed, draws reinforcement from the constitutional structure of checks and balances: power limiting power, interests adjusting to interests. What has made the system often wretched and brutal is its requirement that interests in order to gain entitlements must have power. The poor have interests, but they have no power.

The remedy is that one that distinguishes constitutional governments from others: law. Where the social contract is not and in the nature of the case cannot be self-enforcing through the approximate equality of powers, law must guard interests. We have recognized this with legal protections of civil liberties. We have after centuries of struggle recognized it with legal protections also of civil rights, notably by the Civil War amendments to the Constitution, the Civil Rights Act of 1964, and the Voting Rights Act of 1965 and its extensions. The poor have a legitimate interest in not being consigned to poverty. Let the "market" benefit them as it can.[5] They have not the power to insure that it will, that in the present and the future it will do better for their interests than it has in the past. They require the undergirding of their legitimate interests through legally enforceable claims for education adequate to equipping them for work, and for work itself. They need, in short, firm economic and social rights comparable to those recognized by the juridical norms of most of the western democracies.

Is it realistic to speak of law guarding the interests of a society's weakest? To do so is what, above all, a constitution is for. A constitution, especially a written one, should be and in fact can only be seen as a contract among the people, an agreement by them that they are one political order. We cannot infer or rely upon the consent to that contract of anyone whose political liberty and material security are not valued. The Constitution of the United States has worked because it allowed for general satisfaction of the people who counted. It did that, however, at the price of keeping the millions of its minority peoples outside the circle of those who counted. Those people, the majority of whom are here by reason of original enslavement or conquest, could not prior to the civil rights movement of the 1960s and 1970s have been held to have given their consent. The slow workings of the Constitution made possible the movement. It secured for them after long struggle their negative rights. It is not politically realistic to anticipate that law will now voluntarily proceed to guard their positive rights. The inherent genius of the Constitution is, however, that the negative rights of voting and freedom of speech and freedom from discrimination can exact from law its further necessary protection, for fair shares in the national economic enterprise.

I I I

The work of minority officeholders may in time make a difference to the depressed incomes and living standards of their fellow ethnics. It has not yet. The recent declines in unemployment rates still leave them at historically high levels (they are down now only to pre-Reagan administration numbers), and leave blacks and Hispanics with rates double or more those of whites. No fact threatens the future of America's general welfare more than that jobs added since 1981 have been overwhelmingly at low wages; indeed, almost half of those new jobs provide income around or below the federal poverty line. In dollars adjusted for inflation, all family income has since 1973 crept downward, notch by notch.

Other changes since 1984 have been either retrogressive or, as with affirmative action, too recent to be evaluated. Minority people are not today better housed than they were in the early 1980s, nor are they significantly better served by schools, better protected by the courts and police, better able to break free from ghettoized cultures, better able to set for themselves high goals and realize them. A gain, quite possibly, is that they have produced a spokesman, Jesse Jackson, who forcefully interprets to the nation the pain of those facts.

But they are not painful for all minority people. Just as with our population generally, so do blacks show steadily widening distribution of incomes. More and more blacks are doing quite well; the middle declines; and more and more are doing very poorly.

Changes in our law and practices of affirmative action exemplify the continued hostile posture of the Reagan administration toward civil rights and minority interests. From its first days in office, the administration tried to get the courts to strike down all goals-and-timetables programs, whether court-ordered or voluntary, and to limit relief. The Supreme Court's 1984 decision in *Firefighters Union, Local No. 1784 v. Stotts* seemed to presage a successful outcome to that effort.

In the spring of 1986, however, the Court decisively turned. In three rulings, it seemed to authorize goals-and-timetables relief, both voluntary and ordered, where there is a firm basis for believing that the absence of minorities resulted from past discrimination. The one clear exception was layoffs; reaffirming the specific ruling of the *Stotts* case, the Court has refused to allow layoffs of whites in order to retain minorities hired later under an affirmative action plan.

The decisions left a good many questions unanswered, and the administration has not given up. Changes in Supreme Court personnel could also cut back on the 1986 rulings. But for the near future at least, affirmative action seems safe.

Ironically, the minority poor face a perhaps more serious danger from the prospect of certain reforms which may be advertised as "liberal." The country is obviously being pulled once again toward the quicksands of welfare reform. This is not to be confused—though the political debates will predictably do so—with the elimination of *poverty*, an immensely bigger and more intractable problem. It is also one that cannot be dealt with by altering people's behavior, which is what welfare reformers always attempt, but only by altering our economy's behavior, and the principles that govern it.

Study after study now breaks forth, some from academic or scholarly institutions, some from various political quarters, Republican and Democratic, though they are by and large all written by the same group of economists and social scientists. A notable consensus is developing, both of vocabulary—"self-sufficiency," "social contract," and "obligation" are ubiquitous terms—and of plans. The latter are variations of "workfare," an idea and practice at least 300 years old in Anglo-Americans' treatment of the poor. Unsuccessful though it has always been, it is being brought out again, clothed in new scholarly data.

If the objective is to reduce poverty and near-poverty by some large measure—and not just to discipline the needy—welfare "reform" is not the path. If we set off on it as if it were, we are fated to go through another period of expensive and ultimately failed effort. From similar seizures in the past the nation has drawn back into lethargic resentment against the poor—for not having been rescued. That will be the danger again.

The core problem of the poor—and barely a third of them are "on" welfare—is that they do not have enough money, and they do not have enough money because they do not have enough jobs at adequate wages. Nor will they, through the job training or job search or job "experience" or workfare, find such jobs. "The availability of work for every ablebodied person who really wants a job is one of the enduring myths of American history."[6]

There are two broad paths, and we venture to say only two, leading toward the reduction of poverty and near-poverty on a large scale. One is some form of adequate guaranteed income for all. The other is full employment, through economic growth and, as required, job creation through public works. We advocated this in 1984. Believing that the goal is necessary and that this is the better path to it, we do so again.

Through enormous expenditures, made possible by unprecedented borrowing at home and abroad, the Reagan administration and compliant Congress since 1981 have stimulated the economy, but the pump priming has been mainly through and by the Pentagon. It is not the right kind, for driving an economy that can sustain growth in those goods and services that people here and abroad want. Monetary and fiscal policies, plus job creation as required, should be seen as combined approaches toward ridding the economy of its slackness and directing it toward full employment and away from its recent trend toward lower personal incomes among all but, as is now the case, the upper fifth or so of our people.

In 1984 we said that politics and economics were primary, that without economic advance minorities would not likely shed their other disadvantages, and that without greater political participation they were not likely to progress economically. This is to say that minorities these days need governments to actively and deliberately widen opportunities for them. We still believe that, even in this revival time of the American civil religion of "free enterprise." But as all revivals must, this one too will have its nightfall. We suspect that public opinion is shifting again toward an understanding that, though government may now and then stumble into being "the problem," it is always necessary to solutions, especially where the needs are those of the poor. We thus look forward with some confidence to a time in the near future when the nation's sense of realism about its problems and clarity about its social obligations will return.

If there were full employment, defined customarily as not over 3 or 4 percent unemployment, at adequate pay, and if it included all employable persons wanting to work, the country would still have heavy social and economic shortcomings. They would weigh particularly heavily on minorities. They would include our acres upon acres of bad housing, our struggling schools, and our unhealthy rural economies.

But full employment would render these problems solvable. Without it, they are not.

10

Not by Law Alone: *Brown* in Retrospect

1994

There is little in this article I would change; certainly not its assertion that the era of great reform through litigation is over. The poor and their troubles are with us still, and African Americans, Latinos, Appalachian whites, and American Indians are the bulk of them—what will work for them? The advance of the economy seems not to lift them up adequately. I doubt that the revived idea of "reparations" is the answer. We abandoned President Johnson's "war on poverty," a national effort with a goal and a readiness to experiment in search of the best means. Maybe a Democratic administration down the road will revive and perfect it.

Brown v. Board of Education was 40 tumultuous years ago. It had come 40 years after the start of World War I, which seemed then as it does now a darkly ancient time, whereas 1954 feels, at least to me, hardly more than the day before yesterday. Our own years gallop by like thoroughbreds. A lot, in truth a lot that is awful, has happened these 40 years; much too that can be cherished.

For the world and for the United States, less though than in that previous 40 years. Not so for the South. Neither measured by data nor by memories had it changed essentially in its culture and politics during those two generations. Cars had replaced buggies, and there were fewer, though still many, blacks, and cotton was no longer king. But the feel of being a Southerner had not changed a lot, the region's politics had scarcely been budged, nor the South's ways of going about its daily life. The South had stayed pretty much what it was throughout years of national and world-wide transformation, through two World Wars, the frenetic 1920's, the beleaguered and also nationally rejuvenating 1930's, the European "isms," the Chinese revolution, the collapse of colonialism, the atomic bomb, Korean War, Joe McCarthy and all that, the onset of the Cold War, even the stirrings of the Negro rising through the policies of the Courts and Mr. Truman.

Not so during these past 40. That the end of cultural isolation was drawing nigh had been foretold in 1948, when the unthinkable had occurred: a Democrat won the presidency without the solid South. That same election, while demonstrating that astonishing possibility, was to mean that not again in our time, if ever, would there be a solid South; not a Democratic one, in any event.

Since 1954, the South has thrown in its lot with the rest of the country, and *Brown v. Board of Education* was the opening act of the drama. What led to the abandonment of the old sectionalism and what had kept the South bound into it before was the same: the primacy of race. The earlier felt necessity of subordinating everything to the maintenance of white supremacy was to be presently succeeded by relaxation, in some respects relinquishment, of the old effort. Yet another "new South" was born.

Release from the old self-imposed burden has brought many benefits to the region, ones that go beyond its having, as it were, joined the Union. More to be savored and valued are ones that simply reflect the rightness of the surrender, for such it was. The seven-year-old child who in 1960 desegregated the Raleigh public schools and for the next five years was the only black pupil in his school was in 1993 elected mayor of Atlanta, his brother having in 1992 become state auditor in North Carolina, the first black to win there a statewide election in this century. They are direct progenies of *Brown v. Board of Education*. Histories like this, of which there are a wonderful many, are the sweetest fruits of democracy and a vindication of faith in it. To those once active in the civil rights movement such stories are thrilling.

The opportunities for individual talents to flourish, the end of organized terror against blacks, a more democratic politics, the end of segregation in public places, the freeing of women and men to love whom they will, such have been rewards that a triumphant civil rights movement brought to the South.

Nothing, though, comes without a price. What have we paid? A discerning reader can begin to estimate it by noting what is *not* mentioned above. We would be foolish as well as inaccurate to claim that the black population *as a whole* is economically better-off and more secure, that criminal behavior in which blacks disproportionately participate has not increased, that blacks and whites generally are friendlier toward each other, that our youth of either race are better educated or trained. In perceptions—of blacks as well as of whites—there has been retrogression in all those areas, notwithstanding a scattering of contrary data. It is fair to say that neither in data nor perceptions have the high-bounding expectations of the mid-Sixties come close to realization. It is, of course, entirely another question as to whether these dire conditions, or any of them, are attributable to the new civil rights. It is also possible that without those, things would be as bad, or worse.

Possibly all of those bitter developments could be analyzed and explained in class rather than racial terms. An odd thing it is, that Marxists for long shunned giving any independent weight at all to racial and ethnic factors, while on the other side "free marketeers" are equally reluctant to speak of "class," though by now comfortable with the categories of race and ethnicity. The historic American experience has been permeated by race; but so has it been by class, whether or not we easily acknowledge that.

These theoretical issues are ones we need here only to nod at. Moreover, fashioning a distinction between race and class when so many of the non-white races are of one economic class—i.e., poor—is intellectual acrobatics. What is important for us to ponder is the likelihood that black poverty, black criminality, black and white distancing from each other, and above all the ill-education—in and out of schools—of white and black youth may be outcomes of American society as it has evolved through the century, and not solely the behavioral attributes of the poor.

Again, theoretical questions are best bypassed. Whether the economic structure determines culture and politics or vice versa does not really diminish or exalt its central importance. The economy supports us all, whether well or not so well. Whatever is right or wrong today in American society gets its start and shaping there. When the economy fails the general needs of society, some people are damaged badly. The great legal victories of the 1940's and beyond, typified by *Brown v. Board of Education*, did little to prevent that. Nor should we expect further civil rights litigation to do so. We may be angry over the Lani Guinier affair. At the same time, we should recognize that who is or who is not head of the Civil Rights Division is largely irrelevant to the welfare of the minority poor.

The American economy has, first and foremost, failed to provide enough work. Thus it does not serve all. It does not provide for, has not room within itself, for all our people. Except in wartime, it *never has had*. There are too many of us, and that is not simply a demographic proposition. At any realistically conceivable level of population, a substantial number of us will be unneeded for satisfying the demands of the rest of us, and economists know this even if they do not declare it. There is, however, novelty of a kind that questions not only whether change is progress but whether "progress" is not the enemy. This present economy most especially has far too little room for the young. Young males with strong backs could in the past, except during great depressions, find work somewhere, and here in the United States usually work that would support a family; not clearly so any longer. Young trained men and women could look forward to doing very well, better than their parents; doubtfully so any longer.

Full employment in the United States is not possible (which the economists slyly concede by changing their definition, so that they have gone from 2 percent or 3 percent unemployment to 6 percent or 7 percent as the criterion of a fully employed "work force"—and those latter two words also get their own redefining). There is no precedent or other reason to believe that full employment is possible within our present "free market" structure. Its attainability is similarly beyond belief for the masses of poor living in the so-called "Third World."

Perhaps it is not within any alternative. The globe's economic business, once most of its parts have stepped out of subsistence production, may not by any means need all the globe's people.

When the South in our time joined the Union, it threw millions of peasants—not all of whom were black but most were—into situations they could not master, and within which a growing number—growing because biology cannot be denied—find no hope. People without hope commit crimes. People without hope don't much like other people. Youth without hope don't make good students.

II

Is our America a better place than it was in 1954? Are we Americans a better people than we (or our forebears) were then? Any one person's answers would be presumptuous. Give the questions to pollsters, perhaps. On the other hand, unless we *are* better people, the [answers of those polled] would be intellectually suspect.

I think I'll leave these questions here. There is, still, of course, the lingering question: just as blacks must often have had to ask themselves why the society white people have made is worth integrating with, so the South, from deep within its own historical swamp of moral slothfulness, might wonder about the gains of union. The South is a violent place. It learned to be so long ago, perhaps because a culture organized to serve white supremacy required it to be. In the same way, surely, the violence that dwarfs our region's civility (and the nation's) is substantially learned from a culture organized to serve our national military supremacy. James Baldwin once wrote, "I cannot accept the proposition that the four-hundred-year travail of the American Negro should result merely in his attainment of the present level of the American civilization." Integration, of black and white, of South and non-South, is to be valued, at least by those not party to it, only if humanity itself thereby takes a step forward.

We *knew*, in that dawn of the civil rights movement, that it would, that integration meant progress for the nation, for humanity entire. Such were the hopes, the bright and beloved hopes! Even before the "Movement" days, when all things seemed possible—black and white together, we shall overcome—Myrdal had told us that we essentially could *will* an end to the national pain, by resolving the tension between ideals and conduct, by practicing the "American creed." In law, in countless public rituals, in popular entertainment, in all these many ways we have since declared the historic contradiction overcome. Its harshest edges have actually been. What we found in the aftermath was that the "American dilemma" has taken new form. The dilemma which today cripples our nation is not a moral one—as it had seemed to Myrdal—but basically political and economic.

I know how overlapping all those terms are, and how indeed they circle about and turn into each other. Nevertheless, the basic issues today—and this is so both objectively and as felt or believed by probably most people—are material ones. They are related to hard matters such as the definition of national interests and purposes; to the use of military and economic power; to the tensions between the claims of national security and claims of individual freedom; and to the distribution of power, benefits, and costs within the republic.

Now all those matters may be, one supposes, reducible by analysts to morality, but that is contested ground. No "creed" is there for guidance. Even were one postulated, moral decisions could not settle such issues. Moreover, a nation which has learned well to absolve itself, reflexively, from the consequences of its foreign villainies—such as today's crushing poverty in Nicaragua—is not in its present mood to be looked to for moral direction. This means that the era in which the great events and persons of the 1950's or 1960's began is ended. It was an era within which satisfying change could be accomplished with but a single disturbance of the national structure. That one change was to rid our national law and ideology of "white supremacy," and later, by a natural progression, "male supremacy." That work is done, not perfectly or finally, but done as well as any change gets done and well enough so that the finishing work can be carried forward. The remnant problems and hardships are, however, not likely to be remedied in better than surface ways without deep changes, beginning with a national commitment to a full employment economy. That is unlikely, and of all regions of the country the South may be the most resistant to it. There is, consequently, no principled (i.e., truth-respecting) reason for optimism regarding the next 40 years.

III

The South's politics has become more democratic, but that has too often, and too generally, demonstrated the impotence of democracy for governing in the interest of the "least among us." As in other sections, black political leaders of the South have been able scarcely to make an impress on poverty, poor schooling, civic disorder, and crime. Black mayors have become—and this is a consequence of reformed law—commonplace throughout the region, but they've inherited cities where problems overwhelm resources. As long as the South continues to send to Washington such congressmen as it still typically does, it is pointless to pass the blame for that to the national government. It is, moreover, somewhat non-scholarly (i.e., non-objective) to speak, in the hovering presence of these people, of Southern progress.

The underlying force in Southern politics has not changed. It is, as it has been, conservative and centripetal, and the "natural position" is to be somewhere right of center. Too far to the right, and we have the disgrace of "massive resistance"; to be to the left of center is almost unthinkable. The South sits so implacably right of center that bona fide centrists—a Ralph McGill in the 1950's, a Bill Clinton today—get labeled whatever the time's fashionably bad name is: today, it is "liberal."

Are there not unmistakable signs that this Southern drift to the center possesses blacks as well as whites? Blacks have traditionally felt more comfortable in alliance with upper rather than lower income whites, and in local and state politics (if not as yet national) as often as not stand with them.

A phenomenon of post-1960's politics has been the migration of large numbers of the working classes to the party of their bosses. This has happened less in the South than elsewhere because here that was the traditional location. The South's white working class followed its bosses into the Democratic Party in the 19th century and followed them out of it in these later days. Both times, the enticement was racial: at bottom today, even if today a variety of other social concerns drape themselves in its penumbra. The South rose economically as far as it has after 1954 propelled by the black revolt. It was shaped, guided, and to some measure initiated by *Brown v. Board of Education* and the cases descended from it. The revolt freed Southern white business people from the prison of defending a rotten political order and an indefensible caste system. Free at last they got rich; Martin King, the radical SNCC youngsters, and the white liberals did more for the South's wealthy than had an army of chambers of commerce and corporate lawyers. The question is whether the black revolt—if anything is left of it—can now serve the poor.

Why have the poor not organized, found their leaders, become in the Marxist sense a self-conscious class? Martin Luther King was clearly moving toward that cause before he was murdered. George Wiley was attempting it, with some success, before he drowned. Jesse Jackson is a now-and-then spokesman for it, among his other causes. The American poor remain a mute, formless, directionless mass. Nor are they likely to receive from court actions the legitimizing stamp that opened the passageway for civil rights. Our law will recognize *race* as a legal "class," *gender* too; but it has not recognized the *poor* as such, and likely will not. To the extent, and it is considerable, that a people's advance in the United States requires a legal definition of its hardships or handicap, the poor can little expect to receive the benefit of a judicial response to their needs. There is a glimmer of contrary expectation in those several school districts now under courts' orders to equalize their schools. Resistance is intense, and nothing like the Warren court stands at the end of what surely will be bitterly fought over terrain. Nor, in an historical age permeated and sometimes led by popular "movements," did the poor ever—except fleetingly—become part of one or had their own: the poor could be black or Latino, but blacks and Latinos could not be *poor* and count on being heard.

We have had so many "movements" that they sometimes seem like another "estate," a fifth, beyond the press. We have had the civil rights movement, ethnic movements, women's movements, various peace movements, ones for environmental sanity, consumers, homosexual persons, anti-abortion, abortion rights, planned parenthood, political correctness and anti-same, the "Christian" right—each, and there are more besides, represents a questioning of the authority of the state and the efficacy of the two-party system to deal with what is held to be important by a large number of persons. Sometimes lost among the good results is what seems to be a fact, that if the force of these movements energizes the political process, their multiplicity renders the concern of any one of them less solvable.

The public mind too (if one can speak of such) becomes gridlocked sometimes. So many, for example, new sexual causes have asked for public approval that it must be that many citizens want relief from the demand that they accommodate the new, have retired therefore into sometime churlish denial. Abortion, social acceptance of unmarried mothers, cohabitation of unmarrieds, sleep-over privileges for dates in university dormitories, AIDS, condom distribution in high schools, lowering of the definition of pornography, copulation in most movies, social acceptance of homosexuality—all of this coming more or less simultaneously is quite an overload, hard for many to cope with rationally; or to want to.

The old civil rights movement itself, which once had the strength of clarity, and thus gave supporters and friends fairly simple goals, has that no longer. By and large, white supporters had seen it as a crusade for fair treatment and equal opportunities; in short, for reversal of the overt wrongs they, and their ancestors, had imposed on blacks. Blacks were and are for that, but many, perhaps most, saw the goal as equality of *results* as well. Whites have, now and then, given lip service to that but hardly more than that. When the issue is defined as results or outcomes, the whites' tendency is to regard blacks and Latinos and other ethnic groups as only another among competing claims for their attention and support. Even white liberals, the most steadily supportive friends blacks and Latinos have had, are lukewarm to cool about legislative districts gerrymandered for the "result" of electing more minorities. Such gerrymandering is the clearest example I can now think of where "law," with minimal popular endorsement, is establishing a significant minority benefit. With this, perhaps transient, exception we are back to the "dilemma" noted earlier, that of the inadequacy of law to complete the old civil rights cause of jobs and justice, as the Washington march of 1963 proclaimed.

One of the advantages of legal action, such as the great *Brown v. Board of Education* case, is that a decision comes forth; as a veteran civil rights lawyer once put it to me, the courtroom is the only place in American government where you can ask a question that gets an answer. In legislatures and executive offices, issues get tortured more than resolved.

But in actuality, how real is the decisiveness of courts? It took another decade and a half for *Brown v. Board of Education* to receive its authoritative meaning, and that only after almost continuous litigation. (The culmination was a series of climactic cases spaced between the Virginia case *Green v. County School Board*, 1968, and the North Carolina case, *Swann v. Charlotte-Mecklenburg Board of Education*, 1971.) Cases were after that adjudicated around the fringes, and still are being brought and tried. Even were the current school-equalization cases to receive a Supreme Court's favorable order, that would in all probability be but a stage in near-endless litigation.

IV

Brown v. Board of Education was historic. It ended a near-century of the law's willful disregard of Constitutional rights. In doing so, it reestablished the moral authority of national law. The opportunity that the great decision offered was that the nation's actual Constitution—in an Aristotelian sense of the ordering of a society's parts into a coherent political order—would be brought into correspondence with the legal Constitution. That opportunity was refused by the state legislatures, governors, school boards, and much of the white populace of the South. *Brown v. Board of Education* had declared a legal right. For its effectuation, legislative and executive leadership was required, and in 1954 and 1955 widely anticipated. It was not given. Implementation was forced onto the courts unaided, and often defied, by the political branches of state governments. No band of politicians in American history is more deserving of infamy than those of the South during the ensuing hard years. Politicians who today roar about the federal courts' interference in public schools' policies and administration should be reminded that the courts a generation ago had to fill responsibilities abandoned by their predecessors. The courts did so, using what remedies they could devise, such as busing, which they turned from what had been its customary function of maintaining segregated schools to assisting their desegregation.

What the courts could not do, and cannot, is broad and deep planning for the educational needs of schools when those schools are required to serve equally and inclusively all their children. It need not have happened this way. It was humanly possible for leaders at that time to behave rationally. For long that was hoped for. As late as 1963, nine years after *Brown v. Board of Education*, the Notre Dame Conference on Civil Rights Legislation, comprising a representative number of recognized scholars and lawyers, would focus expectantly on legislation in Congress (in particular, on a by-now forgotten measure known as the Clark-Celler bill) and on local school boards. Not a word on busing was in the conference's report. Similar examples could be noted. The 15 years between 1954 and the Supreme Court's justly impatient decrees of the late 60's and early 70's were years when the South's political failure and irresponsibility ruined the life chances of a multitude of Southern children. They also laid the ground for the South's present-day politics of illiberalism, in succession to its old politics of white supremacy, and the distance between is not much.

One of the reasons for that outcome has been, as had happened a hundred years earlier, the inconstancy of the non-South's attention and commitment. The Southern civil rights movement never transplanted well. Its idealism, its youthfulness of spirit, did not travel without souring. The Watts riot and the civil rights leadership's confused response to it, coming as they did in the euphoria following the passage of the Voting Rights Act of 1965 and the brilliantly intense emotion of the Selma march, extinguished flames that would be hard to re-light.

Our gratitude should grow and deepen, therefore, to those who led the Southern civil rights movement, who gave us the conviction that there *could*, even among us weak-kneed human beings, come to be a "beloved community," who taught us to honor non-violence, who said to us that love is more real than fear.

We have made a holiday of King's birthday, which is only partly a blessing. For how can a holiday be built around a prophet? King stands—will always stand unless we smother him with sentimentality and commercialism—as a voice saying, "not good enough." He was a scourge. All prophets are. He was not dreamy—as the yearly incantations of his Washington March speech want to make him out to be—but hard and demanding. The most important thing about King was that time and again he went to jail. Had he lived many of the same leaders who gush over him now would again surely be putting him behind bars. He was a disturber of the peace. The course of American public life since his murder would not, one feels certain, have led him to lay down his prophet's vocation, to accept things as they have become.

How much different we would be had he lived to continue his work is impossible to say; or had the others struck down in those years. There was a notable quality, not only in King's speeches but in those of the Southern civil rights leaders generally and, just as important, in those of countless preachers and community organizers throughout the black South. Almost invariably, they would give a higher reason for their demands than simply their own needs; they would attach their cause to some other: to the national interest, or the nation's hallowed ideals, or religion, to something besides themselves and their own welfare. This is still so, now and then and here and there, but not so characteristically; more frequently today, meaner reasons are the common coin, as for example the case for better schools is typically made in terms of economic competitiveness. As I've tried to think about this essay, I've reread some pages of James Baldwin. He wrote in that old way, and part of his anger grew out of a fear that blacks, once absorbed into white society, would lose their moral and spiritual edge.

Black Southerners raised a lot of white people, not just or even most essentially in a housekeeping way but morally. The churches of the South may still be (as are those elsewhere) largely segregated, but in those white congregations where the gospel of forgiveness and love is preached, the black presence is there; because it was from it that the white folks learned that religion. Southern white liberals found their values when they came to sense, however imperfectly, the black experience. Change is not always progress, and fewer white youth are today close enough to observe, much less vicariously to feel, that experience.

Brown v. Board of Education was meant to bring us closer. It has not. In that it failed. Law is not sufficient unto itself. Perhaps it was always but a fantasy, to assume that declarations of law could put a bridle on people's prejudices and selfishness, on the Leviathan which is the American corporate economy, on the government's neurotic drive for national power and security. Too much seen today makes us wonder if we were not all drunk with self-deception. The requirements of race relations are essentially that people get along well with each other, and that starts with good manners. Beyond manners are other and greater matters—justice, for example—but courtesy and kindness form the doorway. Blacks and whites are now giving each other too much reason to avoid, to dislike, even to fear, each other; to see each other as undifferentiated types, not as individuals. The stereotypes of Reconstruction days—the black male as rapist, the white male as incurably a would-be "baas" (in the South African term), and women of each race as accomplices or mirror images of their men, are recurring. The one advantage the South used to have was that blacks and whites did at least talk to each other. It is worth everything to hold onto, or recover, that practice.

Cornel West tells us that, "The fundamental crisis in black America is twofold: too much poverty and too little self-love." This doesn't help greatly—most hardships, almost anything but conscription and taxes, can be swept under the second term—but in whatever measure it may be true of blacks it is equally so of whites, who have their own share of poverty and their own struggle to respect, value, and love themselves. Black and white, together still. Public policy can only indirectly help with that struggle, but it can directly act against the disgrace of poverty. In large measure it created it. The poor of the United States stand in relation to the rest of us as do the impoverished countries of Africa and Central America to the wealthy industrial states. We don't know what to do about either, within our present ideologies. The numbers of the world's poor, of our poor, grow; the impotence and indeed disinclination of the governing powers to end their poverty grows too.

So too do the limits of judge-made law. The era of social reform through litigation is winding down. The problem is poverty. The wrongs of discrimination that litigation can attempt to resolve are marginal to that base problem, and their righting will not end it. Statutes can do better, because they can command and distribute money. The problem though will remain: poverty. Law in the past 40 years accomplished what it did by disturbing only one basic element of the established social order: white male supremacy. To go further, the economy's way of distributing its costs and rewards will have to be redirected.

The dreadful 40 years before 1954 did have the blessing of ending in widely shared hope. These 40 since did not. The next 40 will have their chance.

11

What to Make of the Old Civil Rights Movement: A Partial and Partisan View

2000

The United States is at war again. Is it our destiny to be so, again and again? Is this what the Declaration meant by pursuit of happiness? Can happiness be found in a war that we are told may have no end and may have no boundaries? Is domination of the world what American citizens truly want and will?

What is clear is that nothing is or can be clear. Wars are famous for producing unintended and unforeseen consequences. We have seen already—and this is still year one—that the Constitution will bend, and the rights of the natural environment too, and that we stand ready to ally ourselves with whatever foreign tyrants offer furtherance of our battle plans. To ask what will become of the old civil rights movement or to the dreams of ending poverty seems almost ludicrous: Mars will decide. At any rate, I cannot.

By the end of the nineteenth century our nation had decided to be an imperial power, and the twentieth century witnessed huge enlargement of our might. Defeat in Vietnam seemed, if only for a short while, to brake momentum toward a kind of Hobbesian omnipotence— to be so powerful that none can rationally challenge. And in that sort of social and political environment the government only will decide what are the requirements of "national security," before which all other purposes must yield as the government sees fit—including the needs of the poor, the care of our natural environment, and our civil liberties. Maybe that priority has always been there, and the modern *change is only in how zealously it is pressed, or how far citizens are willing to allow it.*

Asked to write "a retrospect and prospect on civil rights," I demurred. I have had to realize that I am not able, especially as to prospects, to offer anything like a definitive theme. Racism, not civil rights—which is first of all a legal value—is today's challenge, and, like most commentators, I have not found the way to get hold of that protean phenomenon. So I settle for seeing matters not in the whole, but in bits and pieces. At its best, the South's civil rights movement held a commitment to non-violence, and a common thread in these reflections is a hope for its revival, a hope that we might move away from the plague of guns, in the hands of individuals or governments, and from the intellectual arrogance that justifies their possession and use.

I am all too well aware of the incompleteness of what follows. It is what from one angle of vision, my own, is to be seen.

■ ■ ■

1. The Southern civil rights movement that we knew in the years between *Brown v. Board of Education* and the election of Ronald Reagan was a political movement that grew from and within the rich soil of personal meanings. It had caught hold of each of us who were absorbed into it where we were, and in one way or another changed us forever. Violence surrounded it, wounding and killing some of its best people, but the violence almost never was its own doing. I do believe it left hardly anyone who once gave it allegiance the poorer, in spirit or mind. It was a disturber of public sloth and slumber and a transformer of persons and societies. It was almost certainly an undiluted force for good.

We who were part of it were lucky Americans. May something like it emerge again to raise the sense of possibility of later generations.

■ ■ ■

2. *Crisis*, the NAACP magazine, in its January/February 1999 issue

reprinted Chapter 1 of *The Souls of Black Folks*. It had been nearly 50 years since I had read the book; why was I so late doing so, for by then this great book was already a half century old; why especially when I was then a teacher of political philosophy?

We debate whether race or class provides better access for interpreting our social dilemmas, but in political philosophy, classical or modern, race is the new problem, class an ancient, even an original, one.

A leading purpose of Plato's *Republic* was to find the way to subordinate economic classes to disinterested virtue. Aristotle, with better practical sense, sought in his *Politics* the same end by securing political power within the middle class, protected from oligarchs and the poor alike. Neither had anything much to say about race, unless to separate Greeks from barbarians. The United States is, probably, now forsaking Aristotle's ambitions for middle class primacy, as our democracy slides into plutocracy. DuBois was perhaps glimpsing that sorrowful end when he saw America as a "dusty desert of dollars and smartness."

That marvelous first chapter established right off one of the truths we all have to embrace: that the perception from within a racial group is on some matters superior to that of any outsider. No white person would have, could have conceived the idea of "being born with a veil and gifted with second sight—this double consciousness, this sense of always looking at one's self through the eyes of others." It is one of those ideas which once enunciated is immediately recognized as factual and true and absolutely necessary. It is worth quoting further:

The Negro

> ... is born with a veil, and gifted with second sight in this American world, ... a world which yields no self-consciousness, but only lets him see himself through the revelation of the other world. It is a peculiar sensation, this double consciousness, this sense of always looking at one's self through the eyes of others.... One ever feels his twoness, ... an American, a Negro; two souls, two thoughts, two unreconciled strivings, two warring ideals in one dark body, whose dogged strength alone keeps it from being torn asunder. The history of the American Negro is the history of this strife, ... this longing to attain self-conscious manhood, merge his double self into a better and truer self. In this merger he wishes neither of the older selves to

be lost.... He simply wishes to make it possible for a man to be both a Negro and an American without being cursed and spit upon by his fellows, without losing the opportunity of self-development.

I have long been dependent on Negro people to illuminate our societal situations, on Douglass, DuBois, Baldwin, Hughes, Ellison, Marshall, King, Franklin, Clark, Lincoln—the names flow on—and on non-intellectuals too, in Southern, and also Northern, circles of hardship. I used the word Negro above—and won't again in this essay—because that is what these teachers called themselves.

I am not sure what improvement there is in the term African American, though it seems now to be preferred by those it identifies and therefore I shall use it. But not without a bit of regret. Those old names—colored, Negro, black—had the merit as I see it of keeping a measure of distance from being undeniably "American." I doubt also that switching about of names much helps in a search for identity, if that is what it is. But I am also aware that I am not the one engaged in that search (I have my own). There already have been too many white people telling other people who they are.

I do suggest that much of the intellectual and emotional self-examination that goes on within the non-white communities of the United States—and not only that of the African Americans—is an endeavor to leap over and dissolve what DuBois said a century ago about always looking at one's self through the eyes of others. That leap has been a declaration of racial independence.

It implies at the same time a responsibility for bringing an African American perspective to our besetting political issues. I believe in integration, but I hope that integration does not have to mean that African Americans are to bring no unsettling, upsetting, radical ideas and perspectives to the nation's politics. So far, since the passing of movement days such has pretty much been the case.

■ ■ ■

3. That a succession of social movements would grow from the soil prepared by the civil rights movement might have been foreseen. No other minority had had a history of collective pain identical to that of

African Americans, but the United States had created during its history more than enough discrimination and prejudice toward our nation's array of discrete minorities; they were poised and ready to be set in motion. The latest of these "minorities" are the homosexuals, women and men.

They are too unlike other minorities to be thought of in quite the same way. They do, however, share at least one characteristic with those earlier aroused minorities: they seem not particularly well liked by their predecessors. Many blacks still regard the Fourteenth Amendment and the civil rights statutes of the 1950's and 1960's as their own singular possession (as the Emancipation Proclamation was). Latinos of their several kinds and Indians have not felt secure enough yet to champion the rights of others.

The women's movement did surely get a strong boost from the Negro revolt, and the cause that the suffragettes and social reformers had much earlier fought gallantly for got new life from the civil rights struggle.

Except among women, my guess is that acceptance of homosexuals is lower within the other minorities than in the general population; at best, it is not noticeably higher. And I suspect that that is so regarding even those many homosexuals within their own groups.

Yet homosexuals test the nation's commitment to equality and fraternity, on which the minorities depend, in ways that are clearly fundamental. If all the great social movements of the second half of the past century are seen as being one massive demand that our society be open to and inclusive of all who live here, then that is precisely the claim of the homosexuals. And just as our civics lessons have traditionally insisted, that American unity rests not on shared histories but on shared law and political values, the homosexual challenge agrees. The civil rights movement and all its successors based their appeals on established law; so too does this newest heir.

The barriers to acceptance are, however, high. One is that whereas other minorities are more or less physically distinguishable homosexuals are not. They are known to others by their own statement, by self-identification.

A second barrier is at least as high; sexuality. Heterosexual men (I would suppose, women too) struggle with their sexual wants and desires throughout much of their lives. So much of who we are, who we are to others and ourselves, is defined in and by that struggle. We who are heterosexual indistinctly recognize that homosexuals are having their own experiences and struggles, *but they are not ours.*

Nor, of course, do we who are white men know with any certitude the concerns and experiences of African Americans, Latinos, or women. White heterosexual men are probably the most privileged social class, but also arguably the one most cut off from the lives of others, their feelings, hopes, and cares. But *knowing* that one is apart from people of other races and colors or from women is not the same as *believing* that there truly are men and women who look very much like other men and women of their race but assert the right, even a legal right, to be accepted as different, simply by declaration of a status.

We may have difficulty in perceiving across racial or gender lines the problems that beset other persons but at least we generally recognize that those persons are there and have somewhat immutable identities. One may be full of prejudice against persons of another race without doubting that they indeed exist and share the planet. Nor do they call me to question my own identity. They don't rival me. Our literature, particularly Southern literature, is full of white men's fear that their women, willingly or unwillingly, would fall to black men, but essential natures were not at issue; only potency. For heterosexual men, there was truth—even comfort—in the solidarity implied in the old adage, that below the belt all men are brothers.

Have either society or individuals gained by the assertion of homosexual rights based on orientation rather than choice? There is, after all, a long and oft admired tradition of homosexual love affairs, freely chosen, going back to classical Greece. Would society come apart if it became commonplace for persons to say that they were homosexual or bisexual or now one and now the other, simply because they want to be? I doubt that it would, though many might find that intolerable; nor do heterosexuals typically see themselves as such by choice. We are "oriented" that way.

These reflections of mine are likely off-the-mark to others. At best, they probably illustrate again how hard it has always been to talk about sex. Those of us who are Christians or Jews have had that difficulty compounded by the maunderings of those men who ages ago wrote our holy scriptures.

My theme is hope, always, for peace. There was no credible hope for peace in a Jim Crow South. There is none in any American social order that is noninclusive. Many among us have difficulty understanding the legitimacy of homosexual orientation, a difficulty that impels some to hostility, even violence. We have not yet got beyond violence in race relations. Is there serious doubt that most racial violence is and has been committed by white heterosexual men? They are the carriers also of the disease of violence against homosexuals.

We heterosexuals have to re-direct ourselves; first have to find the will to do so. Southern whites, especially those of us of middle age or older, had this to do once before. And plainly, it was hardest and perhaps least successfully done by men.

A fact about movements against social oppressions is that once well launched they do not go away. The United States's destiny is to be an open inclusive society. This has been its consistent tendency. The claim of homosexual men and women to be fully and rightfully a part of it will not go away. Nor should it. We—and that means first of all we heterosexual men of all races—will agree with those claims, or else we shall not have a society at peace.

▮ ▮ ▮

4. Writing about the South sensibly in the 1990's, hard enough for anyone to do, is an almost self-sacrificial task for one like myself, who in the 1950's and 1960's saw Elvis Presley as a bad joke, Malcolm X as enemy of the kind of "beloved community" we believed King was directing us toward, saw the Black Power rage as a tragic wrong turning, saw as King had come to see the militarists and plutocrats of the South and nation as the true and real foes, *and still does*, despite being left behind on all those convictions by the mass of today's liberals.

That last separation from prevailing—though happily not the whole of—contemporary liberals is the hard and bitter one. The world can endure Elvis, Malcolm, and all that; shrug off and endure even us pokey ones who keep our distance from them. The plutocrats and militarists are another story. I have the dismayed feeling that the New Democrats of Mr. Clinton's sort apparently think them compatible with the spirit and hopes of those earlier years. They are not.

Serious work was done in the South in those days. The Southern civil rights movement reversed the tides of the South's history. Southern liberals, black and white, carried their share of the fight that ended the war in Vietnam. These years were the South's historically finest hour. Our generation's South, unlike that older one so well interpreted by our historians following C. Vann Woodward, had struggled through the fire and *had not* been defeated. We need to remember the pain of the time. We need to remember the successes too.

African Americans were always the driving power. But they were not alone. Whites, especially white liberals, were everywhere an indispensable part of the great reform, though the histories so far written don't give them much applause. Whites need to identify with, and be identified with, the victory, need to celebrate that "something big happened down here and we were part of it." We need some white pride.

The malignant stereotyping of the 1960's as an era of rampant drugs and sex and excess is an insult to the memory of King and those who followed or were represented by him. They—black and white—stood up against the old South of white supremacy and against an America gone berserk in Southeast Asia. We diminish King's stature when we look away from his radical opposition to that war.

"I knew that I could never again raise my voice against the violence of the oppressed in the ghettos," of our poor and sometimes dangerous and riotous neighborhoods, "without having first spoken clearly to the greatest purveyor of violence in the world today—my own government."

That was King speaking in his great Riverside Church address of April 4, 1967. We have had more war making since the Vietnam War of that time, and more arming of our nation and other nations ("A nation that continues year after year to spend more money on military defense than on programs of social uplift is approaching spiritual death.") I doubt that King would, if still among us, alter his judgment about who is the world's leading purveyor of violence.

We could do with a bit less recitation of his appealing "I have a dream" speech and a good bit more of his prophetic—speaking truth to power—Riverside speech. The inner genius of the Southern civil rights movement was that it pulled back and left bare and exposed for a while the layers of American myth, letting our basic faults of militarism and greed and racism darkly to show their reality.

The present myth-making disparages the resistance to that war and those who avoided it. Mr. Clinton's tormented way of avoiding and George W. Bush's way—whether he sought special treatment or not, somebody did for him—were the sort of things that young men commonly did in those grim times, faced as they were with the life choices that a merciless government was forcing on them, either to avoid being killed or to kill others. Better if young Clinton and young Bush had gone off to Canada and sought help from the ACLU's amnesty program; but young men did what seemed best to them at the time and are not now to be criticized for it. Not everyone can have the interior strength of Muhammad Ali.

Our war in Vietnam was a monstrous injustice. America never wants to admit its injustices. So we now hold the war blameless and impugn and downsize those who resisted it.

Is our late war, of bombs and missiles, against Yugoslavia becoming another in the long line of approved wars? Has our volunteer military service ended the era of young men and women's dissent and resistance to war?

■ ■ ■

5. The health of rights and liberties, and of movements to secure them, depends on the rule of law, and that requires effective government. I sometimes wonder if we are not near the brink of being a nation ungovernable.

- a war in Iraq that goes on interminably, one in the Balkans which all too likely may follow the same course, and with little in the way of defined and popularly understood national purposes;
- a war on drugs in which we keep doing what has consistently failed and will predictably go on failing, while putting more and more of our poorer fellow citizens in prison for long stays and which involves us militarily with other countries;

- a "war" which infests our streets with handguns and crimes of violence and property;
- an increasing arms buildup when we have no likely threatening enemy, except imagined or invented ones, so that we are engaged in an arms race with ourselves;
- a Congress that declines to require observance of the War Powers Act solemnly enacted by a predecessor Congress and willfully ignored by intervening presidents;
- that legislates spending caps and then maneuvers around them;
- a Congress that determinedly refuses to protect the integrity of elections, including its own, from the corruption of money;
- a Senate that has turned its back on nuclear restraints as in the rejected Test Ban Treaty and which lusts to evade the peace protecting ballistic missile defense treaty and a Congress which year after year continues to spend billions of dollars to research, develop, build and buy more nuclear arms and their delivery systems (for what?);
- a Congress and administration which, regardless of party, spread weapons throughout the rest of the world, jealous of our place as principal arms dealer of the world, fueling the warfare of the nations;
- and which while grieving over school yard and workplace shootings by its own example sows violence everywhere our flag flies;
- a government which so far as its public policies manifest has no concern over the ever-widening economic inequality within the citizenry;
- and a citizenry which, in all its diversity, cares too little for the common good to bother to vote.

Except for legislation hotly wanted by corporate powers, as was 1999's banking measure, this government is not to be relied on for reforms; especially not for ones serving the people.

■ ■ ■

6. Here in North Carolina, Latinos now are everywhere one looks. It is much the same elsewhere in the South: wherever there are crops

to be tended or construction laborers needed or meat processing assembly line workers wanted or yard workers for suburban lawns and college campuses—wherever, in short, there are low wage jobs to be had.

The Latinos have brought with them their festivals, music, grocery stores. They have brought new strength to the Roman Catholic Church, and to Pentecostal Protestant ones too. And they have put heavy new challenges on our public schools.

It is as if the South, which failed so badly in its long sharing of the land with African Americans is being offered a chance to redeem itself, to act now better and more justly toward darker and weaker folks. Much of that redemptive task rests, however, on the black South, for that is where the economic competition with these newcomers occurs. How capacious is the South's reservoir of low wage jobs? That is where Latinos are entering and from which not enough African Americans have as yet risen.

The United States historically has provided work and home for other nations' poor. It has been a great achievement. It may have been—it was—accomplished in large part through oppression, exploitation, and cruelty (as we are reminded whenever Columbus Day rolls around) but it has been done. There was always at least a veneer, and a progressively deepening one, of native manners and legal norms that moderated the hardness and gave grounds for the national boast of this being the land of opportunity. The world's poor voted with their feet to come here, and to stay. And those brought here as slaves have overwhelmingly wanted to stay, and to be Americans, as DuBois said long ago. And as all these poor have come and stayed they have enriched the nation.

Until the present day incursion of Latinos the South had had relatively little to do with this assimilation. In this, as in so many ways the South has, since Southern civil rights days, now joined the nation. The Latinos as yet (but it is still early!) have not been a united political force. They have become strong in some widely separated areas: in the Southwest where Mexican Americans have long lived; in Puerto Rican districts of New York City and the northern cities; and in south Florida where deracinated Cubans have muscled onto the rest of us a revengeful policy toward their native land. Probably Latinos elsewhere, including these newer arrivals, will soon shed their political quietism.

But how, and into what? Will these newcomers find common cause with the well rooted and growingly politically strong Mexican Americans of Texas and the Southwest? If so, they could become a powerful political force. Stronger yet if they also moved in step with those who came from the Caribbean Islands.

What will it be like in the coming decades to have no longer just one but two ethnically diverse bottom rungs in the region's society and economy? What might it mean for the usual African American issues, affirmative action for example? What will be the political shape of the South if we have not one but two, all too likely disadvantaged, ethnic minorities? What might Republicans fear and Democrats hope for? Or vice versa?

■ ■ ■

7. Medieval feudalism had a territorial base but had other defining characteristics as well. There are aspects of modern America, all of them strongly noticeable in the South, that are suggestive of a "New Feudalism." Substitute modern corporations for old duchies and earldoms, and there are important likenesses.

There is combat with other corporations, as once there was between feudal lords, the rivalry often ending in negotiated or "hostile" takeovers. There is the procuring of vassals, with terms of fealty imposed or negotiated depending on relative strength. The lords amass immense personal riches, their wealth and power over vassals grow—call the modern vassals employees, subcontractors and suppliers, retained lawyers and advertisers, local dependents—grow so large as to enable challenges to the government itself, and possible control of it. There was and is widespread practice of bribery, often in our time in the form of campaign contributions, comparable to the levies of old kings on their nobles or the purchase of the loyalties of courtiers by granting of favors and privileges.

And, of course, then and now, securing all this is government's readiness to use its weaponry and military strength if necessary, for the crushing of foreign rivals to the corporations of its own domain.

An important difference from the old feudalism is, of course, that there is today in the United States as in the West generally, a large middle class. Will it hold, as the classes above and below it expand?

The alliance between corporation and state power is a part of Southern tradition, culture, and present-day reality. The reluctance of Southern workers to join unions and their general docility are legendary. The South's Protestant churches have been well represented in the merger—for that is what it generally is—of governmental and corporate interests. If now and then churches may find cause to oppose the government, it is far rarer that they question corporate power.

Over the decades, black Southerners have tended to look for political support to the moneyed class in their communities. We are as far now as in the past from that long dreamed of coalition between African Americans and the white working class. There are cultural and historical imponderable causes for that, but also and probably more basic, obvious economic reasons. One aspect of it was to be seen in civil rights days, when in one locality or state after another African Americans saw their goals as winning over the "power structure."

In the 1990's, a new and potentially socially-wounding circumstance has emerged. Throughout the South, white liberals have in considerable numbers taken up environmental causes. In many localities, and the Triangle area of North Carolina is one, environmental protection and its cousin, curtailment of developmental sprawl, have become liberals' chief concern. It is only a casual one for African Americans, and seldom one for the moneyed class.

At least for the present, this tension between African Americans and liberals hardly affects national politics. In many localities, however, the split is sharp and growing. African Americans emphasize the jobs that development supposedly brings; besides, as themselves mostly dwellers in inner city neighborhoods—and many of those not very pleasant—they tend to give little weight to protecting a "way of life" from sprawl.

The moneyed whites as a class are Southern traditionalists; that is, by heritage they are little persuaded of nature's rights, are short-range in economic decision-making and planning, rigid believers in property rights, and subservient to the wills of the chief business powers of their areas. These being also late 20th-century Republican Party values, there has been a natural fit.

African Americans customarily have seen their own economic interests tied in with those of the elite's of their localities. That was not seen, however, as political separation from white liberals. It is possible that liberals' and environmentalists' resistance to the developers and their political allies could yield such a cleavage. If so, how and where will we vassals of the new feudalism turn?

■ ■ ■

8. We Americans are told often that we are the world's chief power. How is that message felt by the citizenry, high placed and low? How do we feel in being superior? Possibly like a Californian comparing himself to an Alabaman? Or a Harvard man, or woman, looking at someone from Podunk State University?

The South's heritage of battlefield defeat set it apart from other regions. Presumably that induced among us a certain measure of humility. Does it still linger, or has it been erased by migrations into and from the South, by Southerners having become "mainstream"? Probably it has. Social scientists have their techniques of weighing and counting but they'll doubtfully find much humility here; nor, in fact in the United States' other sections, West, East, or North.

Certainly not in our capital, which knows that we are the world's shepherd, pastor, mentor, guardian—in short its "number one"—and in need of no other nation's approval or good opinion. The Democrats will usually be a little more courteous than the Republicans in saying so, but for both national parties, however, we are a norm to ourselves. We are the world's leader in power, and therefore may define our responsibilities unaided by other authorities.

Are we independent of God too? or any "higher law" than our own perceived interests? Have we recruited God in their behalf, as Southerners did in slavery times, and just as surely did in the decades that followed?

We expect universal approval of all our ways, and the intentions that motivated them. First of all, we insist on that among ourselves. The war in Vietnam is being elevated to a level of orthodox approval and honor it never had in its own day. Its place in revered history is being proudly secured. The witnessing to the contrary of thousands of our best youth who resisted serving is being lost from societal memory.

We enjoy calling America a peace-loving nation, but it is not. We Americans are not. We by all objective evidence must love war, because in our relatively short history we have had so many. From the War of 1812 to the recently concluded one against Yugoslavia, there have been few years when we were not at war with some people. Indian tribes, Mexicans a time or two, Spain, each other, whomever.

This continual warring has deposited a thick layer of militarism over our culture. So thick and wide, as to cover us all inescapably, falling alike on Harvard, *The New York Review of Books*, *The New York Times*, the Hearst papers, Bob Jones University, the Christian Coalition, the NAACP, the ACLU; all are swimmers in this ocean of militarism.

Nowhere more than in this South, unchanged despite migrations and a stronger economy from its devotion to things military. Our Congressional delegations are the Pentagon's most loyal followers, teammates actually. The editorial pages of our leading papers seldom betray doubts that the military are our proper leaders. ROTC units are in many secondary schools. The presence of the military is visible throughout the region: in North Carolina, and the state is not exceptional, there are three Marine bases, one Army (Fort Bragg), two Air Force, and a Coast Guard base. About 111,000 active duty personnel and more than 17,000 civilian employees are stationed at them. That makes for a powerful bond between the Pentagon and the state's political and business leaderships. What politician ever stands against, even questions, an employer of that size in his or her state?

My pastor when spurring his congregation to greater social concern and activity likes to say "pick up the near edge of some great problem" and take hold of it, at some sacrifice to yourself. If the overcoming of militarism and violence were to be our purpose, there is no better "near edge" to take hold of than our national affection for capital punishment. That fondness is most ardent in the South. The United States leads the Western world and the South leads the United States in this practice that sets us apart from most of Western civilization.

The death penalty is unfinished business of the Southern civil rights movement. It is a massive assault on the poor, discriminatory in application and in outcome.

What else so focuses on our African American citizens; or is so predominantly in all its processes administered by whites? When the civil rights movement, by first targeting on lunch counters in the early 1960's lifted a "near edge," it did not pull high enough to end this violation of human dignity and life.

The Southern movement was dedicated to non-violence. If there could be a movement of re-commitment to that, the death penalty would in near time fall. So might the culture of guns; so might in longer time even our predilection for military solutions to all diplomatic problems.

The great legacy—the history changing legacy of the Southern movement—could be, and in loyalty to that movement and its leaders and workers should be, the spread of the politics of nonviolence.

Now that would be our good new, our good old, cause.

■ ■ ■

9. The old term, civil rights, is not as helpful as it once was. Given its history, it suggests that for the remedying of problems a law needs to be passed or a march held. I think we have very, very serious inequalities in American society and most of them are connected with race. My own view is that they are bred by the economy and by racism. Nothing original in that.

I may be a mite more, if not original at least novel, in admitting right off that I do not have an answer worth sharing for either. It does seem clear that neither laws nor marches are useful. There are, of course, egregious faults of law that from time to time surface and need correcting and racial offenses—police brutality cases, for prime example—that call for determined, demonstrative direct action. But the deep systematic inequalities of our economy and the racism embedded in layered strata of our culture are beyond the reach of those traditional responses.

Another of the many problems for which I have no answer is the schools and in particular the racial cleavages within them. The hours of discussion and planning by school authorities and committees and advisory bodies (and I've been a sometime participant) is matched by the huge federal dollars, beyond anyone's early prediction of need, that have flowed since the Elementary and Secondary Education Act of 1965; there have been comparable state and local dollars. And still throughout the South, including southern and central Appalachia, too many children can hardly read or count. The schools surely can put more money to good use. That is not all they need, however, and probably is not the most important need; but what and how? I little know.

If the Dred Scott decision of 1857, which stripped "personhood" from African Americans, was the foulest action ever of our Supreme Court, the second foulest must be the 1886 decision in *Santa Clara Co. v. Southern Pacific P.R. Co.*, and others like it, which conferred "personhood" on corporations. To that end, the Court used that same equal protection clause of the Fourteenth Amendment that was enacted for the benefit of and has been the charter of liberty for African Americans, and now for other discrete minorities. Unlike Dred Scott, Santa Clara has endured, expanded, and become hardly questioned. Even the ACLU enlarges it, as it fights strenuously for corporations' right to free commercial speech and political spending.

We may not have political democracy for much longer if corporate powers can control elections and the policies of those elected; we won't have economic democracy if these powers of the new feudalism are beyond the public's regulations.

All I feel assured enough about racism to propose is that we—that means white people mainly—learn to recognize its appearance in nearly all we do, and excavate it as we can. But saying that is not particularly helpful. But what has been? I think back to Gunnar Myrdal's famous "rank order of discrimination," which in order of strength among white people ran downward from intermarriage, to personal relations, to public segregation, to political disfranchisement, to official discrimination, lastly to forms of discrimination in earning a living. Myrdal believed that among Negroes the order was almost the reverse; i.e. they cared most about the last, least about the first. Economic discrimination being first for Negroes and of least concern for whites, Myrdal could feel some optimism about the future. Well, it has not worked out that way.

One reason it has not is what Myrdal in later writing termed "structural unemployment" and with it the emergence of an "underclass," "unemployable persons and families of the bottom of society" who are relatively untouched by the upward trend, if there is one, of the general economy. William Julius Wilson has more recently deepened and elaborated this point. As long as our politics cannot get beyond welfare-to-work as a policy for solving poverty the country will not even confront it.

Instead, we shall wrap ourselves in controversy over so-called issues such as abortion—important in itself but, as a political issue a roadblock to those challenges government can in fact do something about—and trivial pursuits like political correctness, whose debaters often seem like intellectual children, jousting on their playground, swatting gnats and swallowing the camels of war and militarism, poverty and racism, and the degradation of nature. It is time to get serious, and to put aside these screens that facilitate our turning away from those problems that truly have our civilization by the throat.

This past October the Raleigh newspaper had a picture of North Carolina's chief justice of its Supreme Court swearing in the newly appointed director of the State Bureau of Investigation (sort of state FBI). The only thing remarkable about the occurrence was that both gentlemen are African American. It is a happy fact that news like this is no longer unheard of. This is the bright side of this "new South." That hard, almost unyielding underclass is its darkest side.

The true end of the Southern civil rights movement would be a truly all-inclusive society, one of bountiful and as near as possible equal opportunities, political and economic. We all share this planet. Pat Watters, in his book *Down To Now*, one of the handful of truly fine writings about the African American revolt, wrote:

> If the movement's best meaning is to live on, we will escape the notion of all-good against all-evil, and escape racial antagonism in the fight against racism. We will fight racism as the cancer that it is in the society and in individuals, opposing it in blacks, just as in whites, in the name of their humanity.
>
> It will be an effort to break out of the economic, social and cultural traps that stunt and make gray the lives of so many people, an effort to understand and change the systems that peril the nation and the world, and most of all an effort better to know and understand and love, first ourselves, and then other people—in short, to

find true integration with society, the environment and our fellow man. And what less, really did the movement seek in the South?

The enduring South, the one that has lasted through the decades and is still with us is not fried chicken, country music, and magnolias, not even our better manners. The South that has reared us and formed us is as it has been a region blanketed by the militarists' spirit, the capitalists', too, and racial division.

But there was always more. That militarist spirit did inculcate and breed a disposition to acknowledge and accept duties. From somewhere within the strands of Southern history and culture there came respect for religion, even if not practiced.

And that racial division, no new thing but so old that its origins were forgotten except through studied recall, had become the fabric from which the region's life was and had to be shaped and got used to, not comfortably but something that could be made do for most and even allow and occasionally nourish the arousal and raising up of talents. Blacks and whites had shockingly unequal shares in benefits and privileges, but that culture blanketing both races did at least produce for all a sense of belonging here, of having a place.

For our present generation, it has meant yet more. It has given us the heritage of possibilities made real, of a "republic of equals" not only as wish but as potential. Inequalities are still the norm in the region, but African Americans of the South did abandon subservience, have become an integral part of the region's political decision making,—and *have the awareness that it had and has been primarily through their own efforts that these great advances were achieved.* The South's civil rights movement created a new society, a better one, rife with possibilities and hope.

We have it in our power now to move toward realizing the deepest intent of the revolutionary spirits of that movement. Our power is not large enough to go all the way. But every generation has strength enough to move some distance from that place where it lives, to move its nation and its culture, for all of which it is present caretaker, toward a less violent, more humanity respecting social and political order. For the generations successor to the Southern civil rights movement that is both possibility and duty.

12

1968: A Reflection

2001-2002

Some years seize our memories. For multitudes throughout the world, 1968 must have been such a year. Certainly it was for me. Events that were shattering the public intersected with and in measure changed my own family's prospects. So amidst epic storms many individuals, like us, were wagering their own hopes for better lives.

I want to recount some of that. I seldom like memoirs and shall do my best to minimize the personal in this essay. I don't know, however, of any better way in a short space to probe for the special quality of 1968 than to write of what I saw, felt, and was a part of. In reviewing and rethinking the year, I had to realize how much went on that I was not part of, how much even of that to which I was close I had mislaid or misfiled in my memory. I kept remembering as I went along. I cannot suppose I yet recalled all—old notes are few and fragmentary. The year was of such cardinal importance because it raised, and then left unresolved, the most troublesome issues of our national experience—and character. If we are to understand who we are today, we can do no better than to look back at 1968, what we did and who we were then.

My 1968 had in fact begun in earnest on the night of December 6, 1967. I had sat in the anteroom of Local Board #10 in Mt. Vernon, New York. My son had come to a decisive reckoning in his struggle with the draft. In later years I was to get acquainted, because I was an active advocate of amnesty for resisters, with the stories of a number of the young men who were tested by their government's summoning them to the war against North Vietnam and would be struck by their manifold responses. My son had been eligible for a student deferment, but with that maddening seriousness of some youth of those years he chose not to apply for or accept one.

He opposed and hated the war, but would not take what he regarded as nonprincipled avoidance. So he had applied for a 1-O (conscientious objection) classification and had written the required statement. Now was to be his first hearing, his occasion, as he saw it, to reason with authority.

That, of course, did not happen. His hearing was brief, ten minutes if that. He was sent out of the hearing room, I was called in, pressed by board members—they all appeared to me to be in their sixties—to prevail upon my son to be sensible, to take the student deferment to which he was entitled. I said that I believed in Tony's sincerity in his stand; he was called back in; I was allowed to remain; after a few more exchanges the board said in effect, "Okay, we'll give you a C.O." Their clerk was called in to prepare the record, she then asked that Tony and I be sent out of the room. In a few minutes, he was called back, told that he was as of then classified 1-A, the clerk having informed these gentlemen that they had no authority to give a 1-O for merely ethical (nonreligious) objection. So with that cautionary lesson in official process there began a succession of appeals to levels of authority that would continue throughout 1968 and would be always a hovering presence in our family life. It would go on in 1969 and beyond; he received the 1-O a short while before the draft ended—long enough, however, for him to have secured an approved alternate service, working with inmates of southern jails and prisons. He continued with that work for another two years, though with the draft ended he was not required to do so.

The 1960s were a many splendored, also a many fouled, time. Too much of its latterly bestowed reputation is drawn from its foul parts. Tony's experience was a vignette of, I think, the splendid side of the decade's youths naive sense of responsibility to self and others. They were the generation of the Bomb, and the best of them had lapped up moral seriousness as vital to life's survival. Thus Tony had asked that draft board to reason together with him—and got a quarter hour or so of its time.

Nineteen sixty-eight was a grim year. The battle for racial justice in our South had never been more intense. The war against North Vietnam was brutal, and brutalizing. The peace movement marched and demonstrated continually, often angrily. There was peace scarcely anywhere. Martin Luther King Jr. was assassinated in Memphis, Robert F. Kennedy in Los Angeles. The Republican party, crushed in 1964, had changed itself into a party of the Right. The old liberal coalition forged during the New Deal came unhinged, and the Democratic party floundered. The Ocean Hill–Brownsville conflict in New York pitted blacks against labor. The Republican Nominating Convention in Miami spawned street riots and two homicides. The Democratic Nominating Convention in July in Chicago was a horror. Jews and Negroes found cause to quarrel. Negroes themselves were beset by factionalism. Deep fissures shook other countries—Czechoslovakia, France, Mexico—and their tremors were felt here.

The War, Part 1

The war was the main thing. The southern civil rights battle was next to it. Everything else that happened in the United States was linked to those fronts, usually to both.

The war went on interminably. It poisoned the national community. It became increasingly hard for persons who disagreed about it to respect each other or to discuss it fruitfully. In the 2000 campaign Mr. Gore said that he had overcome his feelings against the war by reflecting that if he did not go one more Tennessee youth would have to do so. I don't believe that that view would have been given much credence by the antiwar protesters in 1968; they opposed anyone's going, and some among them would have regarded staying at home to oppose the war as a larger service. Because tours of service were relatively short there was a steady influx of returning veterans, not all at once when a big parade might have honored them but in almost routine recurrences. There was not much common ground between those young enlistees, the resisters, and the deferred students. The war sharpened class differences among us.

This was a bad war, fought for bad reasons, and the raw irony was that if it was of advantage to any Americans it was not to the minorities and blue-collar whites who did most of the fighting and suffering. Wars fought for territorial gain or economic interest or fraternally in support of the ancestral home of some of our own people may not be "just" wars but at least are somewhat rational—they have a concrete goal—but the Vietnam War was fought by and solely for diplomatic concepts, in an older usage, for "reasons of state."

Civil Rights, Part 1

At the year's start, February 8, three students of South Carolina State College, in Orangeburg, were shot to death on campus by state highway patrolmen. There had been several days of demonstrations on and near the campus in protest of segregation that was occurring, in spite of the Civil Rights Act of 1964, at a nearby bowling alley. No action, then or later, was taken by the state or local authorities regarding the patrolmen. Charges were brought against nine of them by the Civil Rights Division of the Department of Justice, over the reluctance of the United States Attorney of the district. In November, a Grand Jury had declined to indict. Attorney General Ramsey Clark and the CRD were unwilling to accept that and filed a "criminal information" in December. This was the same procedure used to bring the lynchers in Neshoba County, Mississippi, to federal trial in 1965, over the obstruction of local officials. The result was the same too: acquittal, in May 1969. Orangeburg was decidedly not a good way to begin the year.

The case was to convey still further depressing news to Southerners who had tried to believe that the region had matured into a lessened capacity for cruelty. One of the demonstrators had been a young man named Cleveland Sellers. The authorities had targeted him early as an alleged "outside agitator." Sellers had grown up in a town about ten miles from Orangeburg, had enlisted early in the Student Non-Violent Coordinating Committee (SNCC), had become one of its key figures, and had been active in Mississippi and elsewhere in the South. He was also a draft resister. In mid-1970 he was brought to trial in state court on charges of rioting and was convicted that September and given a one-year sentence (he served seven months).

Two of our ablest journalists, Jack Nelson and Jack Bass, covered the case and had subsequently written a book about it, titled *The Orangeburg Massacre*. They were critical of the performance of the FBI. In what was a somewhat uncommon reaction, J. Edgar Hoover himself wrote to the authors in disagreement. Bass responded, point by point. The exchange made the case against the FBI only stronger.

There is yet more. Mr. Sellers—now Dr. Sellers—is a professor and chairs the African-American Studies Department at the University of South Carolina. He has received a pardon, and has had a term on the State Board of Education. "We deeply regret what happened here on the night of February 8, 1968," said Governor Hodges at a thirty-third anniversary commemoration. "The Orangeburg Massacre was a great tragedy for our state. Even today, the state of South Carolina . . . bows its head, bends its knee, and begins the search for reconciliation."

The War, Part 2

The events of the year piled on each other. In early 1968, the "Dump Johnson" campaign began. I didn't care much for it, wanting to know whose favor it would serve. Now and then I would lunch with Allard Loewenstein (when he wasn't flying off to the Dominican Republic or somewhere else in his continuous righting of wrongs). Al was the campaign's chieftain. But much as Johnson had wronged the republic by the war he also deserves everlasting gratitude for his first term. What led him to turn to war-making and to turn away from the cause of reform he had brilliantly led? His personality perhaps. More important, I believe, the cause was, and is, our culture. I am unsure that any president would have done differently. The question before him was not whether to start a war but whether to continue one already ongoing, one begun by his party. Our culture insists on requiring opponents to yield. The administration's confidence was that each turn of the screw would bring the North Vietnamese closer to quitting. Senator McCain, whose own valor was remarkable, has said that the "wrong side won." If Americans still applaud pluck and dedication and patriotism and bravery against odds, they should acknowledge the greatness of the Vietnamese people and their leader Ho Chi Minh and that the right side did win.

The Americans who were killed or wounded in this war deserve full honor, but a truly honoring country would ask itself "Why?" What did they die for? What was achieved by their sacrifice? Our militarists lament what they call the "Vietnam syndrome," which is defined as a refusal to commit our ground troops again into a foreign action. I, for one, would give thanks for the Vietnam syndrome as long as it may last and give gratitude to the men whose tragic fortunes led us to it. We violated it by our war against Iraq, and have again by warring in Afghanistan and other Muslim territories. Despite the present acceptance of the rightness of the Iraqi war, its consequences and the post-war decisions that directed them—calamitous ones and almost not a good one among them—ought to have persuaded a rational nation not to do so again.

I gave the commencement address in May 1967 at Clark College (now Clark-Atlanta University) and had said (a bit too hard perhaps on northern liberals of the time) what still seems to me essentially correct:

> Martin Luther King is to be profoundly thanked for his refusal to direct his criticism of our Vietnam policies at President Johnson. By so refraining, he may be denying American liberals the pleasure of another Bull Connor to feast and fatten on. We found, when the civil rights movement reached into the North, that too many of the old supporters had not really been pro–civil rights but merely anti-South. If someone else occupied the White House, possibly his policy could help us out of the Vietnam mess. But if he is only able to do that (as President Eisenhower was able to end the Korean fighting), then there will be no relief from the Vietnams of the future. The problem is not Lyndon Johnson, as it was never Bull Connor, and is not now George Wallace or Ronald Reagan. Nor was the problem John Kennedy or even John Foster Dulles (though he did come close to symbolizing the problems). The problem is the use of power, the placement of science and technology in the service of national power, and the absurdity of war as an instrument of public policy. What one confronts here is that the myth of power asserts that power has a right to maintain itself against all other power, and that each holder of power has an absolute right to determine what is required to maintain itself. And this doctrine has set men to slaughtering each other from the beginning of time.

Assassinations, Part 1

The killing on April fourth of Martin Luther King Jr. was death to the spirit. Hope gave way to horror. It would be worse even than the loss of President Kennedy nearly five years before, for then it had been possible to believe that the force of history was with the civil rights movement and that somehow it would not be deterred. And the tragedy of the Vietnam War was as of then barely sensed.

Now as the long funeral march made its way from Ebenezer Baptist Church to the Morehouse College campus where Martin's old mentor Dr. Benjamin Mays would say the words of love and blessing, hope was undefined and hard to believe in. People did recover, of course, but in that week and the ensuing rioting one could only bow one's head, and wait. In life, King had not been treated as more than "first among equals," and sometimes not that. In death, we saw that he had embodied the best mind and spirits of the age. He was its soul. He had done as ancient prophets had who pronounced judgments—and his last couple of years were given to moral judgment of our economy and our warring in Vietnam—and then set before the people the path to redemption and to recovery of God's favor.

Like all persons, King had done things he probably should not have done—may have violated one or more of the Ten Commandments. But there was one he did consistently obey: the first, which is certainly the most widely and frequently disobeyed: "You must have no other gods before me."

King's public career was short: from 1955 to his murder in 1968. To my observation, throughout those thirteen years he served no other god—not the god of racial pride or supremacy, not the god of state power, not the god of communism, socialism, capitalism, or any other ideological *ism*.

As long as there may be people with the courage to "have no other gods," the hope that King raised—the hope that we could here create a society which truly chooses life over death—that hope can still live.

Children

One of the building blocks of President Johnson's "war on poverty" was the Head Start program. Nowhere did it mean more than in Mississippi. Among the first projects created and funded in 1965 was the Child Development Group of Mississippi (CDGM). It became the largest of all Head Start programs. Designed largely by a band of young intellectuals from northern campuses, it rather quickly became a program controlled by the local Negro families it served. In an address of mine in November 1966 at Ezra Stiles College of Yale University, I said that what was so remarkable was that "some of the most trod upon enclaves of peasants in this land had discovered that they are communities, and as such are taking a common responsibility for their children."

This kind of grassroots strength appalled the state's political leadership, and the U.S. Office of Economic Opportunity (OEO) in 1966 found it prudent to defund CDGM, or to attempt to. Determined parties within churches, foundations, and labor defended CDGM. One endeavor of OEO was the creation of a new organization—Mississippi Action for Progress (MAP)—intended to displace CDGM. It was led by the very best of Mississippi's white and black liberals (including friends of mine). More struggle ensued, as CDGM with its "local people" leadership fought against OEO's decision.[1] The story of that contest throughout 1966–1967 is too involved to relate here. It suffices to say that in the course of the fight some but not all of the CDGM centers did get re-funded by OEO and that a new organization called Friends of Children of Mississippi (FCM) sought to serve those left out. FCM had no governmental funds; foundations and church bodies kept it alive, much to the embarrassed consternation of those who had wanted its demise. Peace talks went forward, off and on.

So it happened, that on April 18, 1968, I sat with Marian Wright (now M.W. Edelman), the FCM attorney, and Fred Mangrum, FCM's director, in a conference room in Jackson to negotiate with Owen Cooper, a prominent business man and the chair of MAP, and his attorney and my good friend, Francis Stevens, an end to the struggle—which, praise be, we succeeded in doing.

This was as happy an event as 1968 afforded. A good program was saved—saved to continue to serve poor children and their families, and to grow. From centers in four counties run for 18 months by volunteers, FCM by 2002 has grown to serve 3,900 children in a 15-county area, to give employment to about 750 local people, and to manage a wide range of other social services as well as Head Start. Its administration has been excellent, and recognized as such.

There were other significances as well. It is fashionable to disparage the antipoverty programs begun in the 1960s. Actually, ones such as Head Start, legal services, and Job Corps have shown over the intervening decades that governmental funding when administered cooperatively with people in the communities should be acknowledged as a very worthy modern invention of governance. The growing work of FCM—and other of Mississippi's Head Start programs, such as MAP, which continues to thrive—is good witness to that. (In May 2002, FCM broke ground in DeKalb, the home of former Senator John Stennis— the most determined of CDGM's and FCM's opponents in the 1960s— for a sizable new and well-equipped classroom complex.)

CDGM and FCM belonged to poor people. That set the nerves of federal administrators and state leaders on edge, not so much out of fear or antagonism—though those were the motives of Mississippi's Congressional delegation and its state government—but simply from disbelief that poor people could properly manage affairs and money. CDGM and FCM vindicated the legitimacy of these people and their ability to work within the financial and other regulations of a federal agency.

CDGM and FCM were initially opposed by the NAACP and by most of the established black and white liberal leadership of the state. Sometimes leaders have to be taught by their followers. CDGM and FCM were befriended and defended by an informal coalition of private groups, mostly based outside the South. It was a heartening case of solidarity without paternalism. I don't recall that other elements of the "war on poverty"—Job Corps, Vista, legal services—were ever similarly favored.[2]

Hunger, Part 1

A few days after that Jackson meeting, the Citizens' Committee on Hunger in America[3] presented at a large press conference in Washington its report titled *Hunger USA*. It was based primarily on field trips throughout poverty-ridden locales of the United States by members of the committee and by teams of physicians.

In the spring of 1967, some of those physicians had been recruited to go to Mississippi in order to advise FCM on medical services for the children in its centers. What the physicians—who came to be called in the press the "Field Foundation doctors"—saw so appalled them that they streamed to Washington and especially to the office of Senator Robert Kennedy of New York with descriptions of conditions of hunger and malnutrition they had seen in rural Mississippi. Senator Kennedy along with Senator Joseph Clark of Pennsylvania had already made their own observations on site. What they and the doctors were seeing was what workers in Mississippi and other parts of the rural South knew too well: the changing agricultural economy of the South had left thousands of black Americans malnourished and many near to starvation. The Senatorial hearing which Clark and Kennedy called was dramatic and made the fact of hunger a national topic.

The campaign against hunger[4] which followed could be a case study in how policy that benefits people can sometimes actually be achieved—concerned Senators, support from church bodies and labor unions, good press coverage, and money from a foundation made this happen. In time, the federal food programs, including the school lunch program, were overhauled and vastly improved. Malnutrition still exists in our country, but the conditions that affrighted us in 1967 and 1968 are seldom now encountered. That has been one large accomplishment, possibly the largest of the antipoverty policies of the 1960s and 1970s.

Strangely, the progress made in realigning and reforming federal policies in those years was little due to the White House or the Office of Economic Opportunity and emphatically not to the Department of Agriculture, which administers the food programs. The antipoverty strategy of the administration did not, would not, focus on hunger. Democratic party Senators like Clark and Kennedy, and a year or so later George McGovern, redeemed the party. The incoming Republican administration of President Nixon and especially the work of Republican Senator Goodell of New York was clear-sighted and resolute. In my own statement of August 1968 before the Democratic Platform Committee I said, after reciting that the party had occupied the White House for twenty-seven of the last thirty-five years and had controlled Congress for thirty-one of those years:

For whatever good has been accomplished in this country during the past two generations the Democratic party, therefore, may fairly claim some part of the credit. By the same token, it can hardly escape blame for whatever are the ills, especially for those which over the past thirty-five years have grown worse. And it is a fact that the specific form which poverty takes in the 1960s largely is a growth of your years in power.

Poverty is certainly nothing new in the United States, but what has become the contemporary form of poverty is that which exists with horrible intensity in localized places: the vicious slums of our big cities; the rural Black Belt of the South; the Appalachian Mountains, especially its coal mining areas; and the migrant labor camps, East and West.

I suppose one of the lessons to be learned from all this is, don't count too much on one party. Lessons power-holders might learn are to avoid theory—such as, getting food to people is not the way to end poverty—and to be attentive to facts. An even more basic lesson all should learn is that people have the right not to be trampled on and discarded by the introduction of new technology.

The War, Part 3

I am glad that I lived into my adult years before Mt. Everest was climbed and men walked on the moon. Life seems somehow richer, profounder, when it includes the unattained, even the imagined unattainable. Every erasure of the unknown changes life's horizons, and I believe not always for the better.

Men climb Everest these days to pick up predecessors' trash, littered about. And space is getting its refuse. Immanuel Kant asked whether anything straight could be made of such crooked material as men are, and true eighteenth-century optimist that he was, he answered yes, in possibility. A couple of centuries later in the human odyssey, we have more reason to doubt.

I sometimes wonder too whether Western civilization did not take a wrong turn when it moved into monotheism, in particular, Christianity. Was not an awful price paid when in the early centuries in our era

Christianity became the path chosen by the West and not, say, the philosophy of reasonableness and natural law taught by the ancient Stoics? Whatever, there is no turning back—true turning points are points of closure, though whether they are ones of progress is another matter.

The United States is not the nation the eighteenth century birthed, or hardly the one we "senior citizens" once knew. We became in the last century a so-called world power, inclined sharply toward militarism. Our aggression against Mexico had been like that of the neighborhood bully taking what lay within the reach of his lust, and so was our conquests of the Indian tribes and Hawaii, and so too was the Spanish American War. As do the strong the world over, we discovered noble purposes requiring our aggression. Essentially, though, we just "did it," as a half century later we just "did it" against Vietnam. Historians do not like to accept irrationality, so they contrive possible rational explanations, not unlike our "conspiracy theorists" who cannot accept that the lives of the Kennedys and King could be destroyed by such pathetic human beings as those who slew them. I believe that we created the Vietnam war just because, at that time, making war had become our accepted national mission, and we deluded ourselves with notions of honor. I would like to believe that we are not yet at the point of no return. Maybe, but only if old Kant's optimism is valid.

Poverty and Civil Rights, Part 1

Was the civil rights movement a true turning point in America's national life? Was it more than another chapter in the chronicle of a nation that had committed itself to being a world "power"? That depends on what we make of it. If the enduring legacy were to be a controlling commitment to equality of opportunity for all, to prevailing practice of neighborliness toward all, to respect for the diversity of the peoples of this world, to cultivation of peace and nonviolence—if those qualities become firmly embedded in our national life then the answer will be yes, and we will have forsaken the path of militarism and become a truly good civilization.

But if the movement has caused no deep change in American inequality of opportunities, has not improved the "mutual trust at the heart of the social whole" (the phrase is Bertrand de Jouvenel's), has not helped make America a more peace-cherishing and less violent nation, then the answer may be, at least as yet, no.

And if, indeed, there may be or can be a real turning back from where we are to the ingrained racism that controlled the nation before the 1950s, then shall we have truly failed ourselves and the nation's promise.

From its beginning, it was a singing movement. The songs and the way they were sung, came from the churches, those Negro churches that blessed their people and kept them whole. Christianity may have been a mistake of history, but old Stoics like Epictetus and Marcus Aurelius would never have brought about this kind of spiritual revolt against oppression—nor, on the record, would they have been less likely to be oppressors themselves.

The 1960s began with four youngsters sitting down at an unwelcoming lunch counter in Greensboro, North Carolina, and closed with Richard Nixon's election in the middle years of the war against Vietnam. Although in several ways the Nixon Administration would carry forward Kennedy-Johnson reforms, henceforth from the election of 1968 liberals would come to see themselves as "outsiders," and in fact they were. The very name liberal—noun and adjective—would progressively become for many an epithet of derision, disdain, and dislike. Liberals became suspect, alleged underminers of American political and—even more, moral—virtue. The grand old liberal cause of civil rights was more or less mainstreamed, if imperfectly, but its parentage avoided.

The years after the 1960s would see the steady establishing of the hegemony of militarism and plutocracy in American society. Those became a dominant part of our national structure and even identity. They even assimilate as they need to large elements of classical liberal causes such as civil rights and diversity. It seems that minority, gender, and homosexual rights can live, if not thrive, as well within a plutocratic and militarist republic as in a liberal one.

It is not able with the same success to assimilate environmental values and causes nor the claims of the poor for better shares in our economic wealth. The prevailing doctrine is that these concerns are best served within "market economies" of militarily strong states. But multitudes, internationally and here at home, are not persuaded even though themselves part of an engulfing culture of wealth and power.

It is tempting to think of the Poor People's Campaign as a symbol of entry into that changed culture. It was to have been a second march on Washington, Martin Luther King Jr.'s truly serious one, spearheaded by his Southern Christian Leadership Conference. It withered into pitiful defeat and left almost no achievement behind. With its demise, the movement was henceforth bereft of grand causes.

It had begun in early May (the first band of protestors arrived in Washington on May 12). They came to force the national government to confront and act on the fact of American poverty. They came in the name of nonviolence, of American diversity—all of its poor from all of its races and ethnic groups. They came to make Washington *hear.*

They lost on all counts. Would there have been a different outcome had their prophet and leader lived? I doubt it, though surely there would have been at least his clear voice. King's presence had not, after all, salvaged the Chicago campaign of 1966, his and SCLC's first venture North. As it was, the Poor People's Campaign began to fail almost from its beginning. It had counted on mass arrest, on "filling the jails," on dominating the news, and Congressional politics. That did not happen. Resurrection City, on the Mall where the marchers camped, became an administrative burden, absorbing the leader's energies, its existence hardly mattering to the Congress or President. The meetings obtained in Executive offices had neither style, dignity, or effect. A single issue—hunger—replaced the broad spectrum of issues the campaign had originally advanced, and the campaign added little to the movement already driving that cause. Along with my Board member Carl Holman and a couple of others, I visited the "City" twice. The mud was deep and, as well as we could judge, spirits were low. The leading civil rights organizations, other than the campaign's sponsor, SCLC, largely avoided identification with it. The Field Foundation had been a large financial supporter, probably the largest, and so failure of the campaign did nothing to lessen my gloom or my disbelief in the prospects of turning back, or much delaying, the tide of conservative forces.[5]

Nor did anything else that summer. I remember going up to Cambridge, meeting there with Robert Coles, Pat Watters, and Eric Erikson, high-spiritedly thinking to launch a special advocacy project for children's welfare. That did happen later, but not with the force we had hoped for (though through several starts and restarts, and with other parents joining in, the Children's Defense Fund emerged a few years later and is still going strong today). The year abounded, for me, in contrasting events. The day of our Cambridge meeting, which left me feeling again eager for the future, the Russian tanks rolled into Prague, instructively reminding that the world can be—and often is and will be—a terrible place.

My board decided that it would like at our annual meeting in November to have guests to help us interpret the times, and left to me their selection. I invited Erikson and Julian Bond, fresh from his starring role at the Democratic convention in Chicago. We met that year, as we occasionally did, at Mrs. Field's South Carolina estate, and there in one of the poorest corners of the United States, attended by white-jacketed Negro servants, we in that rich setting for a weekend discussed an agenda which mostly had to do with projects to reduce American poverty and discrimination.

Poverty and Civil Rights, Part 2

In July my wife and I went to Mexico for vacation, our first trip outside the United States except for two or three days in Quebec in 1966. Americans on travel to foreign countries often come home to tell of poverty and distress they have seen, and certainly Mexico had plenty; but I was not focused on that—observing poverty was something I did enough of at home. Now we were on vacation, less interested in noting hardships than in enjoying the country and its people. We did so once as the sole Anglos on a two-day bus trip from Mexico City to Oaxaca with an overnight stop in Puebla.

The day in Mexico City when we visited a great museum (I forget which one) at the National University we struck up an acquaintance with a pair of students, which led to their showing us about for the rest of what became a quite wonderful day. After we returned home, I wrote to both, sending along small gifts of appreciation, but never heard back. I have wondered whether they may have been caught up in the insurrectionary rioting around the University that began a few days after our departure; judging from their conversation with us they might well have been.

It was that kind of a year. Eric Erikson figured in another of its episodes. I was approached by Mitchell Ginsburg, a good man who was then serving as New York City's chief of the Human Resources Administration. He had an unusual request. He felt a need for himself and his principal staff to have opportunity to reflect over their work through conversation with thoughtful outside persons, and Erikson was one of those whom we agreed upon.

A series of dinner meetings was held mostly in early 1969, but the organizing was done in 1968. I don't know what benefit they were to the participants. What this participant learned more deeply was how many difficulties surround the task of administering an immense and maddeningly complicated governmental structure. I have steadily moved toward the belief that knowing how to relieve poverty is beyond government's capability. That does not mean government should not try, and certainly government should deepen efforts to prevent poverty, which I conceive to be something parenthood planning and rigorous schooling could do much to achieve. But just as I know of no evidence that any economic system serves the majority of people better than does modern capitalism, I also know that poverty for a sizable minority is an expected by-product of modern capitalism.

My 1968 was replete too with the bizarre. On the recommendation of an editor at one of New York's mainline publishers, we engaged as "secretary" for these meetings an African American woman he had "discovered" (and who indeed could write excellently) and with whom he had contracted for an autobiography. She took notes at every meeting, showed some of them to me—and they were good—and then while we waited on their full transcription drowned herself in the Hudson River.

That tragedy was at least equaled by one that occurred in Mississippi and was bizarre too in its own way, especially in its denouement. On June 30, Thomas Tarrants, twenty-one years old and a Ku Klux Klan zealot, set off to bomb the Meridian home of a Jewish businessman. He was accompanied by another KKK member, Kathy Ainsworth, a twenty-three-year-old Jackson schoolteacher. It would have been another in a lengthy series of bombings in the state, mostly directed against blacks, but now also against Jews; the synagogue in Jackson had been bombed, its rabbi's home and the synagogue in Meridian as well. Tarrants was a protégé of Sam Bowers, leader of a number of atrocities in the state including the 1964 lynching of James Chaney, Andrew Goodman, and Michael Schwerner.

When the young bombers arrived to plant their explosives they were surprised by Meridian police waiting for them. In the ensuing gunfire, Mrs. Ainsworth was killed, Tarrants was riddled by shots but lived, and a policeman and a bystander were wounded. Tried in November, Tarrants was convicted under an old Mississippi antibombing law (the first conviction under it ever) by a jury of eleven whites and one Negro and sentenced to thirty years.

The police had been tipped off by the FBI, which itself had been alerted by the Anti-Defamation League; the ADL had long operated its own intelligence-gathering program and in this instance had paid informants, Klansmen themselves. The propriety of the FBI and the ADL in effect arranging a murder was little questioned except by Kenneth Dean, the executive director of the Mississippi Council on Human Relations (who kept my phone busy throughout this affair), Jack Nelson, the outstanding reporter and editor of the *Los Angeles Times* who wrote about it extensively, and the *Washington Post*. (Other national newspapers, such as the *New York Times*, virtually ignored the story.)

I saw Tarrants once. Escorted by Dean, I was driving through the prison farm, Parchman. He was reading a book seated in a folding chair outside one of Parchman's units. By then he had already come to be regarded as an especially intelligent man. A Christian fundamentalist before, he was one still, but of a different variety. He became "born again." An unusual group of influential persons, including one of the FBI agents who had helped trap him and a prominent Jewish community leader who had helped raise the informants' pay, interceded for him with the state government. His sentence was reduced, and he married a wealthy heiress, finished college, wrote a book, and became co-pastor of a respected nondenominational church in the Washington, D.C. area.

The Election of 1968, Part 1

I had only one try at influencing 1968 politics. That spring I was invited by Bayard Rustin to attend an evening gathering of liberal Democrats at the Greenwich Village home of Robert Gilmore, a prominent supporter of progressive causes, to discuss the issues surrounding and constraining us. I suppose there were a score or so of us and though I recall the names of a few, they are all, I believe, dead; so I do not ascribe views to them individually. But when after a pleasant supper the general discussion began it became quickly apparent I alone favored McCarthy or Kennedy for the nomination and alone was inclined toward the "community control" side in New York's Ocean Hill-Brownsville struggle. So clear was my isolation and so much was I the focus in the discussion—most questions directed at me—that I wondered if I'd been invited for some special purpose. I never knew, and somewhat fumbling conversations later on were not enlightening, so I let it pass. It is worth recalling as an illustration of how confused liberal opinion was in spring 1968.

My personal involvement in electoral politics was a fiasco. Eugene McCarthy had a speaking engagement in New York, and I'd been asked to host a reception beforehand. The hope was that I would be able to bring in some of the black opinion leaders. I tried. Senator McCarthy came, so did a handful of invitees, but not more than that. McCarthy in contrast with Kennedy did not have the trust of black opinion, and my small effort did nothing to change that.

I probably at this time did not pay enough attention to George Wallace and his presidential campaign; the avoidance was likely mainly from distaste. It seemed to me a sideshow, drawing minds away from 1968's main challenges of war and poverty. In post-1948 years down to the present, a common refrain of Southerners when switching parties has been that they are not leaving the Democratic Party, on the contrary it has left them. What that has largely meant is that too many African Americans for their comfort have entered the Old Party. The modern Republican Party of the South was founded on this exodus driven by racial prejudice. A generation earlier George Wallace's politics almost surely would have played out within the party. I suspect that a similar eruption, if that were conceivable now, would be contained within the Republican Party, which is now the white South's leading party.

Of course, another significance of the Wallace phenomenon was the popularity it had outside the South: less than it was to have four years later, but considerable. Wallace's "American Independent Party" became the era's political vehicle whereby many blue and white collar "working people" could vent their discontents. The frustrations were, in the traditional American pattern, not principally directed at economic superiors but at the perceived social elites. Underlying and sustaining the resentments was the remainder of that historical American pattern: racial division. And in the 1960s and 1970s there was the added factor of the war, a war that many sons of "working people" were fighting while—as was in fact widely the case—many of the sons of those elites were demonstrating against it or evading it on college campuses. In the outcome of an election when turnout was well started on what has been its modern decline, Wallace carried five states and forty-six electoral votes—all in the South: Alabama, Arkansas, Georgia, Louisiana, and Mississippi.

Assassinations, Part 2

For my own part, I never fully accepted Robert Kennedy. I had in the first days of his brother's presidency met with the man but only once, and then with a small group, and had shaken hands with him maybe twice subsequently. I had not liked him. I thought him cold and arrogant. Nor could I overlook his record, dating back to his connection to Senator Joe McCarthy's operation, and, more recently, including his role in putting segregationist judges on the federal bench in the South. But Robert Kennedy came to have a powerful attraction for minority people, and one that extended to many of my friends. I shall never forget a phone call I had from Charles Morgan, the esteemed civil liberties attorney, and John Lewis as they prepared themselves to endure his funeral, and the almost-guilt I felt at not being able to share fully their sense of loss. Morgan, who had been an Alabama delegate to the Chicago convention, later wrote—and I cannot gainsay what he said—"Desperately the party needed Bob Kennedy for he served as an emotionally personal conduit for the young and the poor, the black and Spanish-speaking to their government. But that dream was gone now."

His murder was one more demonstration of the collapse of liberalism. I had been, because of my work in the struggle against hunger, asked by Aaron Henry to speak at the convention of loyal Democrats in Jackson on August 11. I did, but kept my remarks brief—quite brief. This convention had become a test of strength among factions, and I was irrelevant to that. But I was intensely proud of what Mississippi blacks and liberals were doing and achieving.

Cesar Chavez had come to the Field Foundation in May, and in time we made a grant to assist the United Farm Workers with its legal problems, and would continue doing so for several years. Not only did Chavez give leadership to one of the most oppressed of America's peoples—the harvesters of our crops—he was moreover the first strong leader of our Mexican-American people.

Field was at the same time beginning its participation in Puerto Rican concerns in the East, and for several years had been engaged with American Indian tribes and organizations of the West. Especially as the depth and extent of hunger and poverty among the bypassed and sidetracked populations of the republic became more real to anyone who looked and listened, we had tried also to be helpful in small ways to the isolated people of the Appalachian coalfields.

Hard-up blacks of the South, Mexican-American farm workers, Puerto Ricans of New York and New Jersey, American Indians of the West, Appalachia's "forsaken people"—these were the people Robert Kennedy had reached and carried hope to as had no other political leader since Franklin D. Roosevelt. I could not understand his appeal, and felt the lesser for that. The word "charisma" has been cheapened and trivialized, but elevated to its proper meaning I think that probably only Martin Luther King Jr., Cesar Chavez, Robert Kennedy, and—though I do not like the fact—Ronald Reagan have been possessed of it in the post-war era.

Schools

The dramas of the 1960s sometimes made school desegregation, which had been the opening act of the civil rights revolt, an almost overlooked concern. It struggled on however, and new and unexpected issues sometimes arose. Perhaps the single most important, certainly the most divisive, arose not in the South and was not directly involved with segregation.

New York City is so huge that little attention had been given there to desegregation. The issues there were ones of control and administration, and had by the late 1960s evolved into contest, often conflict, between the school administration ("110 Livingston Street") and blacks, and also the teacher's union and blacks. New York has been a bottomless experiment station for educational ideas. After I moved there, in late 1965, I once was influenced by a high national leader to look into "new" and "original" ideas then being implemented in another large city, an excitement that lasted only until some modest research showed that at one time or another they had all been tried in New York, as has virtually every educational scheme that gets proposed. (That city, incidentally, was Philadelphia, which by 2002 has become a worst-case example of public school administration.)

In the 1960s, climaxing in 1968, the New York issue was "community control," and the focus of engagement was the Ocean Hill-Brownsville school district in Brooklyn. Under a charter wrested from the school board a group representative of the community was given considerable control of the district's schools. Control extended to personnel appointments, and that immediately thrust the community board into conflict with New York's mighty teachers' union. Supporters of the community groups included the Ford Foundation and some smaller foundations, as well as prominent black leaders, though others of them thought better of opposing the AFL-CIO. This local action came to have, given New York's importance, national reverberations; it became an ingredient in the stew that the Democratic party was unsuccessfully seeking to digest.

Ambivalent liberals, such as myself, were torn between loyalties. I was generally supportive of the community control position, mainly because of my respect for Kenneth B. Clark, the distinguished scholar who headed the Metropolitan Applied Research Center (MARC), our largest New York City grantee. Clark was an ardent champion. So, when asked midway in the dispute to raise the money to pay for a full-page ad in the *Times* I did so, because I did think that the black parents and their representatives had a weighty point of view that was not being reported and understood. What happened then was interesting. The ad, signed by about fifty well-known blacks, appeared September 20, 1968. By remarkable coincidence, on the reverse side of the page was an ad supporting the union with twenty-five or so signers who included some of the great names of American liberalism. I commented on the division within liberal ranks in an address at the meeting of the National Civil Liberties Clearing House, March 22, which is reprinted earlier in this volume.

Blacks, unions, liberal whites, Jews, Christian church groups—these had composed the cohesive coalition that impelled the liberal reformers of the era and which promised national transformation. The Voting Rights Act of 1965 can be seen as reform's culminating victory. The coalition apparently could not endure winning. The year after 1965 saw it progressively unravel, and in 1968 it came near to being undone completely.

I had one other involvement in the year that did directly concern desegregation, though on the collegiate level. It too was a window on the times. The principal campus of the University of Tennessee was (and is) in Knoxville. In the spring it announced plans to expand its small Nashville branch into a large degree-granting campus. The State of Tennessee already had what purported to be a major university in Nashville, the predominantly Negro Tennessee A & I State University. A Nashville attorney, George Barrett, filed a federal suit to prevent what he argued would lead to the "perpetuation of a dual and racially segregated system of state supported universities." He turned to the Field Foundation for initial financial support, and that was provided. Barrett won in a string of legal proceedings, but justice in the courts of the United States is often delayed; the case ended in an almost complete victory *by a settlement in January 2001.*

Progressive changes come slowly and are always resisted. Black Americans have long known that. So too have other ethnic minorities. The problem can be simply the immensity of need. Well before 1968 it was clear that we did not know how to integrate public schools racially while at the same time providing a good education to all and doing so in ways that are satisfying to parents, both black and white. Long before 1968, urban schools North and South were moving toward segregated enrollments, especially in low-income neighborhoods, on their way to becoming as distinctly one-race—African American or Latino—as they had been prior to 1954 and are typically today. Residential patterns, home backgrounds, competitive attraction of private schools, the general support of church bodies for a segregated education within a segregated society, retreat of the federal courts from accepting their responsibility to overcome fully the regime of segregation they had encouraged during the seven or eight decades after the Civil War, the indifference of Congress and continued resistance of state legislatures, and certainly a large measure of prejudice, all of these reasons have actively militated in favor of separation of children from each other. The question for coming years will be whether amidst our militarized, oligarchical society there will be care to change that; or whether the resegregation of the schools is accepted, and the fight that brave plaintiffs and brave black children of the South—Thurgood Marshall, Jack Greenberg, and their lawyer colleagues, and the white ladies who stood with them—are to be repudiated in our times.

Hunger, Part 2

I said above (in "Hunger, Part 1") that perhaps the greatest achievement of the antipoverty programs of the Johnson and Nixon administrations has been the struggle to eradicate hunger and malnutrition as inevitable attributes of poverty.

The appalling Third World–like conditions we of the Citizens Committee on Hunger in America, a few Senators and their staffs, and some reporters saw—in the Mississippi Delta; in South Carolina's low country where worm infestation of children's bodies was a not uncommonly observed fact; all throughout the South's Black Belt, in the mountains of Eastern Kentucky and through southern and central Appalachia generally; on American Indian reservations of the Southwest; in the barrios of Texan cities—no longer prevail.

The gains were not easy, and, in particular, certain southern Congressmen fought tenaciously against them. To be forced to "prove" a connection between hunger (unadmitted) and poverty (undeniable) may seem surreal, but we were made to do it. Congress did in late 1967 establish a National Nutrition Survey under the Department of Health,

Education, and Welfare. Luckily, an outstanding Public Health Service officer, Dr. Arnold Schaefer, was selected to head the project, carried on throughout 1968 and into 1969 and 1970. The Survey provided the documentation relied upon by Senator George McGovern's "Select Committee on Nutrition and Related Human Needs." The survey's findings became an embarrassment to the government, and its reports were blunted before release, which McGovern complained about to President Nixon, and Dr. Schaefer was in the summer of 1970 quietly transferred to the Pan American Health Organization. But the case for Congressional actions on food stamps, on school lunches, and on other programs had been made.

The War, Part 4

So too had the case for withdrawal from Vietnam been made, but against all reason and national self-interest we—the nation—would not officially admit it and would prolong the war for another six years. It would be presumptuous of me to try to add to that case; it has been so well made by others more able. Our son's resistance to the draft went on, as resistance did for numerous other young men, and like many of them he gave his primary interest to work in the poverty-afflicted areas of the South. But apart from attending a couple of meetings I had no active role in 1968 (I did, before the war ended, especially in the demand for amnesty for resisters).

McGeorge Bundy, whose work as a foundation executive I had come to admire and respect but who had earlier been one of the principal inventors and architects of the war, made a speech on October 12 which foretold how the war would be absorbed into American values. As reported the next day in the *Times*, he said, "We must begin to lift the burden from ourselves"—not a word of the burden on the Vietnamese. We must do so not from "moral outrage or political hostility to the objective, but rather on the simple and practical ground that this escalation will not work and that continuation on our present course is unacceptable." The speech can stand for the intellectual elite's refusal to accept blame by denial that there is blame. The nation, he was saying, must get out of Vietnam without damage to those who got us into it. There was more of the same. The "basic purpose of our forces in

Vietnam [is] the purpose of preventing defeat." It was this kind of thinking that made others of us wonder if our leaders had gone mad.

But its deeper meaning has seeped into our national consciousness: we have no need ever to forgive ourselves or to be forgiven. Apology seems to have become something the nation is lately called on to do for various grievances and occasionally is so inclined; perhaps a later generation will apologize for the wrong done the Vietnamese.

The Election of 1968, Part 2

I had in 1968 the good luck to be near the center of three good causes: the defense of Head Start in Mississippi, the campaign against hunger, and voter registration of blacks throughout the South. I had been a founder of the Voter Education Project, at the Southern Regional Council, which under a succession of extraordinary leaders—Wiley Branton, Vernon Jordan, John Lewis—led in the democratization of southern politics.

A good argument could be made, I believe, that in 1968 and in the years since down to the present the participation of southern blacks in the electorate has been the saving strength of the Democratic party—and, therefore, whatever its value is to the republic. At the Chicago Convention the southern delegations, leavened and driven by blacks, were the margin of decency—neither followers of Mayor Daley nor of the street demonstrators—and in the November election they voted strongly. That Chicago convention was not, incidentally, a total disaster. Not only were the Mississippi delegations of Loyal Democrats and half of that of Georgia seated but "the unit rule," which had in the past contributed so strongly to the South's heavy effect in the Democratic party, was repealed.

This essay began with a personal reflection, and ends with another. I wrote for the fall number of *Katallagete*—the magazine of Will Campbell's Committee of Southern Churchmen—an article rather pretentiously titled "A Shipwreck's Survivors." I did not quite say there that in the imminent election I would not vote, but that was pretty clearly implied. And I did not. I did say in the piece that the choice would not simply be between Humphrey and Nixon, and in that I was correct; the choice would be "whether the government is to be headed by Hubert Humphrey, limited and restrained by a Republican opposition, or by Richard Nixon, with a Democratic opposition," and that choice I would leave to others. I was shamefully wrong to be one of the too many to do that.

The decade that had begun so promisingly—I am dating from the Greensboro sit-ins—ended with Richard Nixon. The bright possibilities that I and a host of other believing, hope-indulging people had allowed ourselves to envision would not again in the decades to follow seem so attainable. Liberalism would henceforth be too concentrated on *stopping our leaders* for its adherents to believe in a new national life: *stop the war, stop the arms race, stop the ravaging of the environment, stop the lawlessness of the Nixon administration*—always so much to stop. The negative took over. New frontiers and great societies receded from our horizons.

A Summing Up

Does that have to be our verdict on the decade and its capstone year? In considerable part, yes, but not entirely. There were seeds planted that could return the nation to that which is positive, that which could mean a fuller unfolding of the "New World."

The dominating themes of 1968 had been the war and civil rights. It is neither naive nor unreasonable to believe that despite all that went wrong on both fronts, there can be net gain. If as a result of the travail we are less ready to go to war again, that would be an historic gain for civilization. And the civil rights struggle brought the possibility that—for the first time in the nation's life—government by the consent of all the governed could be a reality.

Much happened in 1968, of course, that brings these possibilities into doubt but not yet extinction. For a mess of oil, the war against Iraq betrayed the first, and militarism was and is invigorated, and probably irresistibly so; but possibly not. The civil rights advance seems much more secure, but that could be because civil rights for minority peoples and women are all too compatible with militarism.

On the dismal side, the election of 1968 brought southern Republicans fully into the Republican tent: on the way to becoming its leaders, not just its ranks. To myself, there seem to be merely stylistic differences between these Republican leaders (except that now women are included) and those who in the years before the civil rights revolt dragged the South into its sordid ways from their chieftainships of the Democratic party. Trent Lott would probably not see or care to admit much difference between himself and John Stennis— nor would I. Jesse Helms is but a craftier "our Bob" Reynolds in a somewhat different style.

For those Southerners who in the years after the war worked to unseat this sort as southern political leaders, it is sadly hurtful to see them now as national leaders.

This is a Republican party committed, as were the old Dixiecrats, to the interests of the wealthy and the Pentagon. To have contributed so lavishly to that outcome is the saddest meaning of the election of 1968. A not inconsiderable part of responsibility for that rests upon those of us who were blind to its likelihood.

When the revolt of the Negroes created the true possibility of a government open to all, other minorities and—above all—women came in too. We have become a far truer democracy than ever before. Whether the democracy we have become can or will want to bridle the militarism and plutocracy—always latent in the American nation, but never before as strong as now—is the question on which all depends, for us and the world.

Can domestic tranquility be long enjoyed amidst growing inequality of wealth and income, which statistics tell us convincingly is a fact? Can world peace be a real possibility when a few nations are favored above all the rest, and their advantages seem to grow? Already there are wars everywhere, killing and destroying and producing hordes of displaced persons who are carriers of new wars. Wars always have done these wrongs, and now do so with immensely greater weaponry, from the supply of which the advantaged nations profit.

A word dear to the 1960s was "empowerment." I have not much liked it, because the "for whom?" has always been murky or unpalatable. But the world, and the United States most of all, will be foolish if it misjudges the depth of discontent with present-day distributions of power and wealth. Protests can be, and often are, crude, rough, mistaken in focus. They don't arise from nothing, however, anymore than did the turbulence of the 1960s. We don't have the spirit and voice of

Martin Luther King Jr. to teach that lesson to us, and the flickering flame of hope and courage lit in the 1960s lost its brightness in 1968.

The world seems awfully big, too big for men and women nurtured in the old traditions of liberalism to direct or much influence. We seem so puny. Corporations swallow up each other in orgies of avarice, monstrous salaries are paid to the few at the top, foundations and a few universities grow incredibly rich, and the richest national states, with their wealth and their guns, try to manage the world.

The ugly and fearsome shape of the future seems so obvious that the burden of proof has to be on those who deny its coming. Aristotle taught that gross inequalities of wealth could not endure. That was a first lesson by the schoolmaster of our political traditions. It demands to be heard again.[6]

Notes

Introduction

I would like to thank some of the individuals who have known Leslie Dunbar—the Rev. Mel Williams, Dr. Sam Cook, the Rev. Will Campbell, Professor David Rothman, Steve Suitts, and the Rev. Joseph Harvard—for their insights. I am particularly grateful to Professor Charles Bussey at Western Kentucky University for sharing his unpublished essay on Dunbar.

1. Leslie Dunbar to author, September 1, 2001, copy in possession of author.
2. Ibid.
3. Leslie Dunbar, *Reclaiming Liberalism* (New York: Norton, 1991), 15.
4. Carol Polsgrove documents Dunbar's role in her book *Divided Minds: Intellectuals and the Civil Rights Movement* (New York: Norton, 2001), pp. 214–16. Dunbar supported Silver by arranging legal assistance when Mississippi officials went after him in the wake of his speech and book publication.
5. See David J. Rothman and Sheila M. Rothman, *The Willowbrook Wars* (New York: Harper & Row, 1984).
6. "Excerpts from *Minority Report*," this volume.
7. Leslie Dunbar, *Reclaiming Liberalism* (New York: Norton, 1991), p. 73; *New York Times* 5 March 1992. By 1987, economist Frank Levy was able to document with meticulous detail the general impact of the Reagan tax cuts in his study, *Dollars and Dreams: The Changing American Income Distribution* (New York: Russell Sage Foundation, 1987).
8. Dunbar, *Reclaiming Liberalism*, 73–74.

9. See, for example, Mary Edsall's essay, "White Suburbs and a Divided Black Community," in *Chain Reaction*. That decline takes into consideration all earned income, direct welfare, housing assistance, food stamps, and the total actual estimated value of medical assistance. The disparate impact of the 1960–1990 period on the black middle class and the black poor is a major conclusion of Hugh Davis Graham in his study, *The Civil Rights Era: Origins and Development of National Policy* (New York: Oxford Univ. Press, 1990).

10. "Excerpts from *Minority Report*," this volume.

11. Dunbar, *Reclaiming Liberalism*, 83, 43.

12. Ibid., 83.

Preface

1. See, for example, Jim Lewis's account, *The Gulf War: The Churches and Peacemaking* (Raleigh: North Carolina Council of Churches, 1997), especially chapters 3 and 4.

2. The other, he said, is "be kind." See Meiklejohn, *What Does America Mean?* (New York: Norton, 1972), pp. 22ff.

3. Against terrorists or possibly their alleged sponsors; perhaps Iraq, for example.

1. The Annealing of the South

Previously published in the Virginia Quarterly Review, volume 37, number 4, Autumn 1961.

1. Editors respectively of the *Atlanta Constitution, Norfolk Virginian-Pilot, Arkansas Gazette, Gainesville* (Georgia) *Times,* (South Carolina) *Cheraw.*

2. Civil Rights and Civil Duties

An address to the Catholic Interracial Council, New York, 28 October 1962, in days immediately following the Cuban Missile Crisis. Copyright © Southern Regional Council. Reprinted in New South (November–December 1962): 10–15.

1. I can no longer recall the name of the magazine.

3. The Changing Mind of the South: The Exposed Nerve

From the Journal of Politics, Blackwell Publishers, February 1964; reprinted in *The American South in the 1960s* (Praeger, 1964), and also in large part in *The*

South and the Sectional Image, edited by Dewey W. Grantham, Harper & Row, 1967.

    1. W.J. Cash, *The Mind of the South*. N.Y., 1941. W.A. Percy, *Lanterns on the Levee*. N.Y., 1941; the quotation is from p. 286 of the 1959 reprinting. James Agee, *Let Us Now Praise Famous Men*. N.Y., 1960; the book was written in the late 1930s. Lillian Smith, *Killers of the Dream*. N.Y., 1949; revised edition 1961.
    2. Edited by R.H.S. Crossman, N.Y., 1949.
    3. Gunnar Myrdal, et al., *An American Dilemma*, N.Y., 1944, p. 27.
    4. Myrdal, op. cit., p. li.
    5. There has been a lot of recent writing on this subject, mostly by non-southern interpreters. See the three books of essays by James Baldwin: *Notes of a Native Son*. Boston, 1955; *Nobody Knows My Name*. N.Y., 1961; *The Fire Next Time*. N.Y., 1963. Essays in the first book are of uneven quality and interest, but some of them and all of the two later books are superb and required reading for insight into the Negro revolt. For the latter reason only, so too is Louis Lomax, *The Negro Revolt*. N.Y., 1962. See also the excellent book by Harold I. Isaacs, *The New World of Negro Americans*. N.Y., 1963. Isaacs has an especially interesting essay, in *Encounter*, August 1963: "Blackness and Whiteness." One scientific inquiry is B.P. Karon, *The Negro Personality*. N.Y., 1958; its findings and methods aroused some dispute. As a stranger to psychology I hesitate to cite writings in this field but from a dilettantish reading I might mention three pieces which were suggestive to me: Robert Coles, "Serpents and Doves: Non-Violent Youth in the South" (in Erik H. Erickson, ed., *Youth: Change and Challenge*. N.Y., 1963); Lewis W. Jones, "Negro Youth in the South," (in Eli Ginzberg, ed., *The Nation's Children*, Vol. 3, N.Y., 1960); D.C. Wilson and E.M. Lantz, "The Effect of Culture Change on the Negro in Virginia, as Indicated by a Study of State Hospital Admissions," *American Journal of Psychiatry*, July, 1957.
    6. A. Schumpeter, *Capitalism, Socialism, and Democracy*, 3rd edition. N.Y., 1950, p. 143. Schumpeter's brilliant analysis (pp. 121-64) around the theme of capitalism's "crumbling walls" illuminates racial unrest throughout the world. As capitalism sponsored its own intellectual and emotional opposition, so European-American culture has sown the denials of its own privileges.
    7. Ibid., p. 145.
    8. *Taylor v. New Rochelle*, 195 F. Supp. 231, 294 F. 2d. 36 (1961).
    9. See chapter 4 of the *Manpower Report of the President and a Report on Manpower Requirements, Resources, Utilization, and Training*, U.S. Department of Labor, 1963. The statistics above are from *Statistical Abstract of the United States*, 1962, p. 215, except for the 1963 ones, which come from news reports.
    10. See Charles E. Silberman, "The Businessman and the Negro," *Fortune*, September, 1963.

11. The ability of southern Congressmen to act through concepts of the national interest, so long as they felt presently secure in race relations, made possible the reforms of Wilson and Franklin D. Roosevelt. For an interesting case study, see I.A. Newby, "States' Rights and Southern Congressmen During World War I," *Phylon*, Spring 1963.

12. cf. the interesting analysis by Gerhard Loewenberg, "The British Constitution and the Structure of the Labour Party," *American Political Science Review*, September, 1958.

13. Which is, of course, being supplied. The point of view I have here expressed is consistent with that of Allport and his supporters. See, e.g., Thomas F. Pettigrew, "Personality and Sociocultural Factors in Intergroup Attitudes: A Cross-National Comparison," *Conflict Resolution*, March 1938; and "Regional Differences in Anti-Negro Prejudice," *Journal of Abnormal and Social Psychology*, July 1959. From the former: "The success of the movement in the South does not depend—this hypothesis would contend—on changing the deeply ingrained orientations of prejudice-prone personalities; rather, it rests on the effectiveness with which racial integration now going on in the South can restructure the mores to which so many culturally intolerant southerners conform."

14. Delaware, Kentucky, Maryland, Missouri, and West Virginia have all legislated some minimal standards and mediation procedures for racial relations, and the governor of Kentucky has gone further with a sweeping executive order.

15. I have been privileged to read a draft of the forthcoming book of James McBride Dabbs, whose *The Southern Heritage* (N.Y., 1958) is the likeliest candidate of recent years to stand beside the classic interpretations of Cash and Lillian Smith. Dabbs has *not* tired of the search.

4. An Excerpt from My Foreword to *Climbing Jacob's Ladder: The Arrival of Negroes in Southern Politics*

Foreword from Climbing Jacob's Ladder: The Arrival of Negroes in Southern Politics by Pat Watters and Reese Cleghorn, copyright © 1967 by Southern Regional Council, Inc. and renewed 1995 by Southern Regional Council, Inc. Reprinted by permission of Harcourt, Inc.

5. Remarks to the National Civil Liberties Clearing House

Remarks to the National Civil Liberties Clearing House, in Washington, D.C., 22 March 1968.

1. Bantam edition, pages 481–82.

6. Remarks to the Mississippi Council on Human Relations

Remarks to the Mississippi Council on Human Relations, 30 April 1975.

1. The psychiatrist Coles, author of many books, was active in the South's struggles; the preacher, pastor, and author Campbell has been one of the constant guides for the rest of us.
2. Joyce A. Ladner, *Tomorrow's Tomorrow: The Black Woman* (Garden City: Doubleday, 1975), pp. 97–98.

7. Remarks to the Southern Regional Council

Address to the Annual Meeting of the Southern Regional Council, Atlanta, Georgia, 3 December 1977.

1. Martin Luther King Jr., "Room in the Inn," *Bennett College Social Justice Lecture Series* 2 (fall 2000): 6–7. Used by permission of Bennett College.
2. *Chicago Sun Times* 12 November 1977.
3. *St. Luke's Journal*, University of the South (June 1968), p. 43.
4. Ralph C. Thomas III, Statement of the Harvard Law School Committee on Military Justice before a subcommittee of the House Committee on Veteran Affairs, 27 June 1977.
5. *Identity, Youth and Crisis* (New York: Norton, 1968), pp. 290–91.

8. The South: Then and Now

Address at the Southern Education Foundation's Conference, 3 April 1978, in Atlanta, Georgia (on the occasion of John A. Griffin's retirement and Elridge W. McMillan's installation).

1. John Ehle, *The Free Men*, N.Y., 1965.
2. *Southern Justice*, ed. by Leon Friedman, N.Y., 1965.
3. J.M. Dabbs, *Civil Rights in Recent Southern Fiction*, Atlanta, 1969, pp. x–xi. Dabbs had once been a member of the Southern Regional Council.

9. Excerpts from *Minority Report*

Minority Report: What Has Happened to Blacks, Hispanics, American Indians & Other Minorities in the Eighties (New York: Pantheon Books, 1984; revised, 1987).

1. John Rawls, *A Theory of Justice* (Cambridge, Mass.: Harvard University Press, 1971), p.102.

2. "A major national goal for this decade should be to arrest the proliferation of disadvantaged female-headed black families. Family reinforcement constitutes the single most important action the nation can take toward the elimination of black poverty and related social problems." *A Policy Framework for Racial Justice* (Washington, D.C.: Joint Center for Political Studies, 1983), p. 12.

3. Walter E. Williams, *The State Against Blacks* (New York: McGraw-Hill, 1982). The Sowell shelf lengthens. His positions are well enough stated in Chapters 5, 6, and 8 of his latest: *The Economics and Politics of Race* (New York: William Morrow, 1983).

4. For one aspect of this, see Elizabeth Drew, *Politics and Money* (New York: Macmillan, 1983).

5. A lengthy two-part article by Christopher Jencks evaluating blacks' recent economic experiences concludes, perhaps not very helpfully: "It is hard to see why blacks should sacrifice themselves on the altar of competition when hardly anyone else shows any inclination to do so." *New York Review of Books*, March 3 and 17, 1983.

6. Michael B. Katz, *In the Shadow of the Poorhouse* (New York: Basic Books, 1986), p. 6.

10. Not by Law Alone: *Brown* in Retrospect

Previously published in the Virginia Quarterly Review, volume 70, number 2 (Spring 1994): 205-19.

11. What to Make of the Old Civil Rights Movement: A Partial and Partisan View

Previously published in Virginia Quarterly Review, volume 76, number 2 (Spring 2000): 236-54.

12. 1968: A Reflection

1. John Dittmer's term, in his fine book, *Local People* (Urbana: Univ. of Illinois Press, 1994).

2. Of the several Head Start programs of 1965-1968, the two that have grown to become the largest in the state are MAP and FCM.

3. Dr. Benjamin Mays and I were the co-chairs. The committee had been convened by Walter Reuther of the United Auto Workers.

4. The story has been told often, most vividly by Nick Kotz, *Let Them Eat Promises: The Politics of Hunger in America* (Englewood Cliffs: Prentice Hall, 1969).

5. Two good reports written at the time were: Warren Pritchard, "The Poor

People's Campaign," in *New South*, then the magazine of the Southern Regional Council (fall 1968), pp. 2 and 21; and Calvin Trillin, "Resurrection City," *New Yorker*, 15 June 1968, p. 71.

    6. Aristotle. *Politics*, Book 4 (and throughout).

www.ingramcontent.com/pod-product-compliance
Lightning Source LLC
Chambersburg PA
CBHW030639150426
42813CB00050B/188